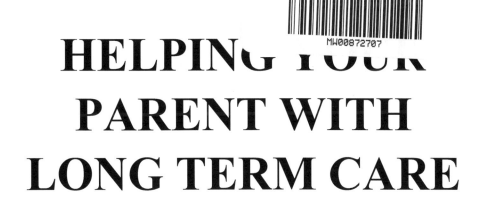

HELPING YOUR PARENT WITH LONG TERM CARE

Texas Medicaid Eligibility

&

Strategies to Save The Estate

By

Taylor Phillip Willingham, J.D. M.S.

Estate Planning College
3900 S. Stonebridge Dr., #1101
McKinney, Texas 75070
www.estateplanningcollege.com

Printed in the United States of America

First Edition

Dedicated to Bad Financial Advisors

You failed…my turn.

TABLE OF CONTENTS

ACKNOWLEDGMENTS

Thanks to my family for suffering through the time it took me to put this book together. To my hundreds of clients and Adriana Shade who have struggled with me while dealing with Texas Medicaid Program. I hope this book will help those in the future understand the difficulties in dealing with Texas Medicaid Program. Also, to my amazing employees who keep The Willingham Law Firm running: Kellianne Beechly, Carla Alston, Dian Hartel, Cindy Galvan, Samantha Gremminger, Vedhasree Periathambi, Ben Russell, Michael Adams, Rachelle Dytko, and Brittni Bell.

In addition, I would like to thank the many attorneys who have spent decades of their life passing on their wisdom. Some of those individuals are: Scott Scolkoff, Wesley E. Wright, H. Clyde Farrell, Patricia Flora Sitchler, and Molly Dear Abshire. Your books, education material, and lectures have assisted me greatly in my practice. Last, to Jeffrey Reddick for providing his wisdom and writing the last two chapters of this book.

Note to the Reader

This book is designed as if I'm speaking to a daughter about her mother's elder law needs. I designed the book in this way because it is the most common situation I face.

MEDICAID LINGO & TERMINOLOGY

"Community spouse" is a husband or wife of a Medicaid applicant who qualifies as a community spouse. Two requirements are necessary for your mother or her spouse be considered a community spouse: First, your mother or her spouse must be married to the "institutionalized spouse," meaning the one who resides in a medical institution or nursing facility and is "likely to remain there for at least 30 consecutive days." Second, the community spouse cannot also be receiving long-term care in a medical institution or nursing facility.

"ICF-IID" is a facility with a certified designation from Medicaid to provide for individuals with intellectual disabilities. These facilities are called "Intermediate Care Facilities-Intellectual Disability."

"Medical Effective Date" is "...the date on which the individual is eligible for medical assistance under the State plan and would otherwise be receiving institutional level care...but for the application of the penalty period."[1]

"Medicaid Long Term Care" is the author's terminology to refer to Texas Medicaid long-term care services and community-based support services. This program is run through Texas Health and Human Services

---

[1] 42 U.S.C. § 1396p(c)(1)(D)(ii)

Commission (HHSC). HHSC oversees three departments: (1) The Department of State Health Service ("DSHS"), (2) The Department of Aging and Disability Services ("DADS"), and (3) the Department of Family and Protective Services ("DFPS"). DADS is the department responsible for Medicaid Long-term care and for the administration of the Medicaid Estate Recovery Program ("MERP"). The DADS webpage is www.dads.state.tx.us.

"Texas Medicaid Program" is the Texas Medicaid Program run by Texas Health and Human Services Commission (HHSC).

INTRODUCTION: ETHICAL CONSIDERATIONS TO GOVERNMENT BASED LONG-TERM CARE PROGRAMS

The design and structure of this book is to assist you or your loved one as you explore long-term care planning options available through the United States government. To simplify this book, I'm writing as if I was speaking to a daughter who is in the process of helping her mother. Many of the clients with whom I have worked have encountered this very situation. It seems that traditionally daughters are the ones who assume such a role in respect to their parents and usually, the mother lives longer. No offense of course is intended towards those sons who take care of their fathers and/or mothers.

When referring to your mother's spouse, I will not refer to him or her as your parent, as many elderly people do in fact remarry. While it might appear awkward to refer to your parent as "mother's spouse," please understand it is intentional.

Long-term care options are typically divided into three categories: (1) personally financed long term care, (2) third party financed long term care, and (3) government-based assistance. These represent the different types of financially structured living arrangements that exist today. This environment however, is constantly evolving to keep pace with our national needs. So, while this book intends to be a comprehensive overview of the government-based option, Medicaid, one should always consult with an attorney before proceeding with any sort of long-term care planning, particularly that which involves government-based assistance.

It is important to understand that in engaging the government to pay for your mother's care, you should be mindful that the government is really a reflection of our national community. We simply aren't a society of unlimited resources. Therefore, when the government pays for your mother's care, it is actually your neighbors, friends, children, and yourself who are paying. That said, keep in mind that our nation can only survive when each individual member takes responsibility for whatever he or she can. While it might be too late for your mother to finance her long-term care, you should attempt to take care of your potential future needs.

As a country, we firmly believe in loving our neighbor and helping those who require assistance; this is who we are, this is what makes this nation so dynamic. The government has thus put into place a program for long-term care managed under Social Security laws. In addition, the United States also has a program for veterans, widows of veterans, and their disabled children known as Aid & Attendance Pension Benefit. However, this book will not focus extensively on this particular program. Rather, I will review the nuances of the Medicaid system and how best to navigate it when caring for a parent or loved one.

Understandably, the concept of Medicaid and all that it entails can be fairly confusing. This is why I will do my best to be as direct and as simple as possible regarding the components and ideas involved. The goal is to focus primarily on Medicaid and its long-term care which is available in Texas. While some of these concepts will apply to most states, each state runs its own Medicaid Program under the direction given through federal law.

In order for your mother to qualify for Medicaid nursing home care or a waiver program, she must meet three criteria: first, she must have a medical necessity for which an individual seeks government help; second, she must meet income requirements in order to receive assistance; third, her assets must be below the required amount set forth under Medicaid rules.

While most people who are reading this book may be tempted to avoid the Medicaid Estate Recovery Program period, a few might wish to repay Medicaid after they pass away. If your mother does not like the idea of having the government pay for her care, she might still want to obtain Medicaid benefits. Your mom can structure her estate so that she qualifies, but ultimately allows the Medicaid Estate Recovery Program (MERP) to recover expenditures. Outlined below are benefits you receive by qualifying for Medicaid even though Medicaid will be paid back after you pass away.

Qualifying for Medicaid will have the following benefits:

(1)   Medicaid pays about 15% to 20% less for most services than you would have to pay privately.

(2)   Eligibility for a Medicaid program (such as nursing home Medicaid or the Community Based Alternatives program) that pays for prescription medications qualifies you for membership in a Medicare Part D plan that covers such medications without paying a premium.

(3)   It may be many years until your surviving family members have to pay back Medicaid, and no interest is charged on this kind of "loan."

(4)   It is possible that your estate might avoid estate recovery because your beneficiaries have taken steps to assist the decedent which lowered the cost of care.

As an attorney it is not my job to determine whether it is right or wrong for someone to take Medicaid. It is my job to help them navigate those legal services available to them.

Often there is confusion regarding legality when it comes to the transfer of assets for the purposes of attaining Medicaid. On January 1, 1997, it purportedly became a crime to knowingly and willfully dispose of assets in order for an individual to become eligible for Medicaid, if disposing of the assets results in the imposition of a period of ineligibility. Enforcement of that law has been enjoined in *New York State Bar Association v. Reno*, 97-CV-1768-TJM-DRH, (S.D.N.Y.). However, to this day no one has been criminally charged for transferring one's assets to become eligible for Medicaid.

My last concern involves financial advisors. Understandably, a financial advisor is someone you trust, someone with whom you've probably developed a relationship over the span of a number of years. Their job is to manage your money, and so when a daughter of a long-time client calls informing said advisor that all of mom's money has to be moved, the advisor is extremely hesitant to proceed with such a transfer. Frequently, these advisors will in essence step in the way of planning. There will thus be push back on their end—as maintaining their clients and managing those clients' money is how they earn their living. For each hundred thousand dollars held under management by a financial advisor, that generally translates to a thousand dollars a year in revenue. So, moving money can cost an advisor tens of thousands of dollars over the course of a decade.

On one such occasion, I informed an advisor that we had to move a client's IRA to a certain type of annuity. Out of professional respect, I allowed him to see if he could in fact execute this transfer. I however, knew his company would not allow this. Of course, as expected, he informed me that his office refused to let the assets be moved to such an annuity. I tried to explain that this was in the best interest of both the mother and the father, as this

15

particular annuity made it so that the mother qualified for Medicaid and consequently, kept the father from becoming impoverished. His response to me was that I should, "keep drafting wills and trusts" and he would handle the finances. The clients took his advice. After losing hundreds of thousands of dollars, they returned to my office to do the plan. In part, this book is dedicated to that advisor and the many advisors out there who failed to help their client prepare for a long-term care situation. Also, I don't want to throw all financial advisors under the bus. Many of you have spent countless hours trying to convince your client to prepare for this situation to only have your client reject your plan.

DOCUMENT OVERVIEW: COMMON DOCUMENTS DRAFTED BY ELDER LAW ATTORNEYS

1. **Durable Power of Attorney** – a document authorizing an agent to act on behalf of a principal by conferring certain powers. This power of attorney can be "springing"[2] or effective immediately.

2. **Medical Power of Attorney** – a type of durable power of attorney which authorizes an agent to make health care decision for a principal.

3. **HIPAA Authorization** – The Health Insurance Portability and Accountability Act (HIPAA) provides for federal protection for individual health information. This authorization allows an individual the power to disclose personal health information about said individual to another.

4. **Out-of-Hospital Do-Not-Resuscitate Order (DNR)** – This document is prepared and signed by an attending physician who, with the patient, directs initiation or continuation of cardiopulmonary resuscitation, advance airway management, artificial ventilation, defibrillation, transcutaneous cardiac pacing,

---

[2] Texas Estates Code § 751.002 – A springing power of attorney becomes effective after a certain event takes place, like one's incapacity. While this might sound like a good idea, it is often hard to implement because of the difficulty of getting an individual deemed incapacitated.

and other life-sustaining treatment.[3] Documents can be obtained at www.dshs.texas.gov by typing the name in the search bar.

5. **In-Hospital Do-Not-Resuscitate Order** – This document is the same as an Out-of-Hospital Do-No-Resuscitate order, but this is done in the hospital and placed in the individual's medical records. An Out-of-Hospital DNR is not effective in a hospital.

6. **Declaration of Mental Health Treatment** – This form, which is only valid for three years, allows an individual to direct mental health treatment.[4]

7. **Declaration of Guardianship** – An individual can have a written statement directing who will be his or her guardian of an Estate or Person if the individual is deemed incapacitated.[5]

8. **Disposition of Remains** – A disposition of remains is unnecessary unless an individual does not want the following succession of individuals to control the disposition of his or her remains:[6]

    1. The surviving spouse of decedent;
    2. One of the surviving children of the decedent;
    3. A parent of the decedent;
    4. A sibling of the decedent;
    5. Any relative who is in the closest degree of kinship as determined by the laws of descent and distribution.

---

[3] Tex. Health & Safety Code Ann. § 166.049
[4] Tex. Civ. Prac. & Rem. Code Ann. § 137
[5] Tex. Estate Code § 1002.12
[6] Tex. Health & Safety Code Ann. § 711.002(a)

9. **Directive to Physician** (also known as a "**Living Will**" and "**Advance Directive**") – a document which authorizes administration, withholding, or withdrawal of life-sustaining treatment if an individual is in a terminal or irreversible condition of a qualified patient.[7] This document is often confused with a DNR, but it is very different.

10. **Last Will & Testament** – a legal document in which a testator expresses their desire to distribute their property and designate an executor to manage the estate until property is distributed. Historically, "will" referred to real property and "testament" applied to disposition of personal property. This distinction is no longer used.

11. **Living Trust** - a guide to property where you give control over the property to a Trustee and the beneficial interest to a beneficiary. This guide explains how your property should be administered and distributed to another. Often in the context of Elder Law, a Living Trust is created to avoid probate. However, the government has placed restrictions on the use of such a trust in order to gain access to Medicaid Long Term Care.

12. **Qualified Income Trust** - or a "**Miller Trust**" is a trust used in "income-cap" states where the state requires an individual to have a Qualified Income Trust if an individual exceeds the income limit for Medicaid Long Term Care.

---

[7] Tex. Health & Safety Code Ann. § 166.031(1).

13. **One to Four Family Residential Contract** (resale) -TREC - This is the most common contract used in the state of Texas to buy and sell real estate. This document is used to purchase a homestead for someone who might desire to shelter some assets in case they end up on Medicaid Long Term Care.

14. **Personal Caregiver Agreement** - an agreement among a caregiver and a recipient which provides compensation for a caregiver in exchange for services offered to a recipient. Due to the nature and abuse of Caregiver contracts, Texas Medicaid places many rules upon the use of such contracts.

15. **Supplement Needs Trust** – a third-party trust created by an individual for the benefit of someone who is disabled. Usually these types of trusts were created to protect assets passed to a disabled individual so said person could still maintain their government benefits.

16. **Special Needs Trust** – With passage of OBRA in 1993, a self-settled trust (first party)[8] allows an individual to place his or her resources into a trust for the purpose of qualifying for government benefits. Often this is allowed if the State recovery system is the remainder beneficiary on the trust.

---

[8] 42 USC 1396p(d)(4)(A)

PART 1: NURSING HOMES & MEDICIAL NECESSITY

CHAPTER 1: THE BASICS IN ASSISTING YOUR MOTHER

Never make your mother's situation worse...Often many people come to me after making serious errors because they did not want to hire an "expensive attorney." Most attorneys who practice in Elder Law will save their clients far more money than they will ever spend on that attorney's services. An Elder Law Attorney can sometimes save you hundreds of thousands, even millions by showing you precisely how to shift financial responsibility and reduce the cost of care.

One issue which comes up frequently and which definitely should be addressed, is when it comes to gifting on your mother's behalf. If your mother does not have the mental capacity to make a gift, then any such gifting strategy which we pursue could ultimately be considered invalid. The strategies as far as gifting go will thus depend upon your mom's mental condition.

I often have children who come to me explaining that he/she has "gifted" his/her mother's money to him/herself. The line between a gift recipient and a thief can be quite blurry when dealing with the elderly. As you will see later in this book, gifting strategies are difficult and need to be planned out

Helping Your Parent with Long Term Care

carefully. Please do not gift your mother's property to any person without having your Elder Law attorney review such gifts first.

Failure to act is often the most serious error that I have seen in terms of Elder Law planning. When your mother's mental capacities are declining the situation almost never improves. However, many of my clients hold on to the belief that their mother will be just fine, that she will improve and that all will go back to "normal." And so, after spending a great deal of money, they finally seek out assistance only to discover they are too late to do the essential planning needed. I have also seen clients who decide to do nothing, often instigated by their fear of making a serious mistake, not realizing that inaction *is* the mistake. It is critical that you take ownership of your mother's financial situation and put her needs above your own; in this way, you will almost never go wrong.

An important note: If you are acting as a power of attorney on behalf of your mother, it is my opinion that you should always act to preserve your mother's estate. In accepting the authority granted under your mother's power of attorney, you establish a "fiduciary" relationship with her. This unique legal relationship imposes on you certain legal duties, and these duties will in fact continue until you resign, or the power of attorney is terminated, suspended, or revoked by your mother or by operation of law.

A fiduciary duty generally includes the duty to:

24

(1)   act in good faith;

(2)   do nothing beyond the authority granted in this power of attorney;

(3)   act loyally for your mother's benefit;

(4)   avoid conflicts that would impair your ability to act in your mother's best interest;

The key concept here regarding power of attorney is the obligation to "act." Failure to act and thereby in some way cause serious financial harm to your mother, is a violation of your duty. It is important to always remember that certainty is illusory. If you are attempting to do your best to assist in your mother's financial situation, you will not be held liable as long as you follow the four principles above.

Another common error I unfortunately see when a child is preparing their mother's estate for a long-term care situation is the selling of her primary residence. Under Medicaid law, a primary residence is not considered a countable asset towards Medicaid eligibility. While selling a property and paying for her care *might* ultimately be the best decision, she may desire to one day return home. However, if you have opted to go ahead and sell the property, your mother will probably never have an opportunity to purchase a residence again and therefore, will have no home to which to return. Not to mention, in almost every situation I have come across, the individual desires to leave their home to their children. For many people, a home represents their largest lifetime financial achievement.

Just as gifting on your mom's behalf can be tricky, you also need to beware of giving your mother gifts. After your mother is eligible for Medicaid, if you or anyone else gives her anything which is considered "income," Medicaid places a requirement that it be reported to them; if this new "income" raises her above the "income cap," she will be disqualified for benefits. The Medicaid income limit is $2,205.00 per month (as of 2018)—although the amount changes at the beginning of each year. Income is considered cash paid to your mother or property that can easily be converted into cash. In addition, they count any payments to providers of food or shelter for her benefit.

Sometimes it may be easier to understand what is not considered income. As long as someone pays a third party for anything other than food and shelter, then it will not be considered income to your mother. For example, if you took your mother to the movies, paying for her ticket is not considered income. However, if you purchased her popcorn, then you would have to report it to Medicaid. Maybe, let her eat out of your bucket.

While we have not yet talked about a "waiver" program, it is important to note that gifts of food and shelter are not income when on a Community Based Alternative program. To make matters even more complicated, it is counted as income to a person who is on a Community Care program. Later in this book, we will talk more about these programs. At this time, just note that if you are concerned about understanding the line between income versus non-income, make note of this so that you remember to discuss it with your attorney.

Lastly, if your mother has long-term care insurance and qualifies for Medicaid, your mother might want to apply for this program to help pay for prescription drugs. This way she will benefit from the Medicaid rate and also have the long-term care insurance pay for her care. Keep in mind that sometimes long-term care insurance will not cover the entire amount. If this happens to be the case, your mother's income will then go toward paying for her care and her spouse will get to keep the rest of the income. This also could be a great strategy if your mother's spouse is in a nursing home and has long-term care insurance. Also, as Medicaid pays for all of your mother's medications, this helps bring down the cost of her care even further.

With Medicaid funded programs, a person must be a resident of the United States in order to receive benefits. What's more, your mother must be a resident of the state in which she is seeking Medicaid assistance. As parents age, it sometimes makes sense to move them closer to you. This is absolutely fine, just keep in mind however, that residency needs to be established. So for instance, if your mother has been living outside the United States, she must be here for at least 30 days. In Texas, your mother has to establish Texas residency and show that she intends to stay here. Your mother is considered a resident if she establishes an actual dwelling place in Texas. You can prove residence with property, income or other tax forms, a lease agreement, or utility bills.[9]

---

[9] Tex. Admin Code § 358.207

CHAPTER 2: WHAT IS MEDICAID LONG-TERM CARE?

T exas Medicaid program is a federal/state funded institution that is governed by the Texas Health and Human Services Commission. It is a program designed to assist the aged, blind, disabled, and impoverished families. It is often confused with Medicare. *Medicare* is an insurance program which each working American earns after obtaining a certain number of credits. *Medicaid* is a welfare program based upon medical need, income and resources. Medicaid long-term care or Medicaid-Institutional and Community Care programs assist with paying for long-term care needs in a nursing home, intermediate care facility if your mother has an intellectual disability or related condition, and institutions which cover those 65 years and older who have mental diseases. Medicaid does not usually pay for an assisted living facility (however, Assisted Living and Residential Care Services is covered under a Community Care program) unless it meets one of the requirements above. I promised that I would try to keep this as simple as possible; basically, what you need to understand is that Medicaid is what pays for long-term care when your mother does not have the assets or resources to pay for herself.

You need to first understand that Medicaid may not be for everyone. For example, you may not want to take part in a Medicaid program if (1) you morally disagree with welfare, (2) Medicaid-certified homes do not provide you with the opportunity to be in your own room, (3) you might want to live at an Assisted Living Facility, or (4) the law changes making it so that if you plan to gift away your assets you are thus barred from Medicaid.

Some important programs to be aware of:

1. **Medicaid Waiver Programs** -- These programs are designed for your mother if she decides to stay home instead of going to institutional care. These programs usually have a waiting list. Often this is a more desirable program because your mother could live at home and have someone come in to assist her.

2. **Medicare Savings Programs** -- This is a Medicaid program that pays Medicare cost-sharing expenses.

3. **Primary Home Care** – This provides for personal assistance services to a person of any age who has a functional impairment when it comes to the ability to perform daily activities.

4. **Family Care** -- This provides for personal assistance services to individuals who are not eligible for Medicaid-Funded primary home care services. These services can be meal prep, cleaning, shopping, laundry, and transportation.

5. **Home-Delivered Meals** -- This program provides nutritious meals to individuals who are impaired and who have limited assets and income.

6. **Assisted Living and Residential Care Services** -- Often referred to as "supervised living," this service is offered to people who need access to 24-hour care but who do not live in a nursing home.

7. **Day Activity and Health Services (DAHS)** -- This is an adult day care program.

8. **Emergency Response Services** -- A service which provides electronic monitoring systems.

Yes, there are numerous options for your mother's care. Do not feel overwhelmed. You don't need to become an expert on the various Medicaid funded programs out there. Once your mother applies for benefits, a Medicaid employee will determine which programs she receives.

Medical Necessity

While your mother might meet the income and resource requirements to be eligible for Medicaid, she still might not meet the Medical Necessity requirement. "Medical necessity" means, in general, that your mother requires assistance (more so than with just the daily activities of living) from a registered or licensed vocational nurse on a regular basis for a disease or medical condition. This requirement applies to Medicaid institutional benefits (care in a nursing home).

The actual rule is found in Tex. Admin. Code § 19.2401, "To verify that medical necessity exists, an individual must meet the conditions described in paragraphs (1) and (2) of this section.

(1) The individual must demonstrate a medical condition that:

(A) is of sufficient seriousness that the individual's needs exceed the routine care which may be given by an untrained person; and

(B) requires licensed nurses' supervision, assessment, planning, and intervention that are available only in an institution.

(2) The individual must require medical or nursing services that:

(A) are ordered by a physician;

(B) are dependent upon the individual's documented medical conditions;

(C) require the skills of a registered or licensed vocational nurse;

(D) are provided either directly by or under the supervision of a licensed nurse in an institutional setting; and

(E) are required on a regular basis.

In order for a nursing home to receive any money from Medicaid, the facility will have to fill out an MDS assessment. This Minimum Date Set assessment gathers the information necessary to determine whether or not your mother has a need to be in a nursing home. If you believe your mom might not have a medical necessity to be in a nursing home, you can go online, download this form and see the questions that will be asked of her.

A Community Care program on the other hand, does not require that your mother have a "medical necessity," but does require that your mother is disabled to the extent that she cannot work. In addition, your mother must have a score of at least 24 on the "Client Needs Assessment" questionnaire. For your mother to qualify for such programs, her countable assets must be below $2,000 (or $5,000, depending the program which is involved). However, your mother can qualify immediately by transferring assets (there are no transfer penalties which apply to these programs). This planning can be difficult. While there might not be a penalty for transferring, there is a waiting list to get on some of these programs.

Also, keep in mind that while your mom might qualify for Medicaid benefits, she has to find a facility which has a "Medicaid bed" available. It is no secret that the government pays less—usually as much as 20% less for your mother to stay at a nursing home. It is therefore often difficult to find a good Medicaid nursing home which does not have a waiting list.

CHAPTER 3: STAYING HOME AND OTHER HOUSING OPTIONS

M ost of my clients want to stay home as long as possible. The government also understandably wants your mother to be able to stay home if possible. Why? Because it costs the government a lot less if your mother is not in a facility. There are two different types of programs which offer care to the elderly at home. One is financed through Medicaid, the other is financed through Title 20 (block-grant) funds.

Title 20 (Block-Grant) Fund Programs

If your mother desires to stay home, the three major programs which could assist her are: Family Care, Primary Home Care, and Community Attendant Services. There are a number of services they could provide for your mother. However, it is fairly difficult to pre-plan what services will be offered to her. First, she will have to undergo an assessment interview; this in turn, will determine how many hours of services she receives. The hours will be between 6 and 41. If she needs more than 41 hours, Medicaid will require that your mother be placed into a nursing facility or assisted living facility. Remember, in order for her to qualify for this program she will have to score at least a 24 on the "Client Needs Assessment" questionnaire.

Client Needs Assessment Questionnaire

Here are some of the questions they will ask her:

1. Do you have any problems taking a bath or shower?
2. Can you dress yourself?
3. Can you feed yourself?
4. Can you shave yourself, brush your teeth, shampoo and comb your hair?
5. Do you have any problems getting to the bathroom and using the toilet?
6. Do you have trouble cleaning yourself after using the bathroom?
7. Can you get in and out of your bed or chair?
8. Are you able to walk without help?
9. Can you clean your house?
10. Can you do your own laundry?
11. Can you fix your own meals?
12. Can you do your own shopping?
13. Can you take your own medicine?
14. Can you trim your nails?
15. Do you have any problem keeping your balance?
16. Can you open jars, cans, bottles?
17. Can you use the telephone?

18. During the last month have you often been bothered by little interest or pleasure in doing things? Have you felt down, depressed or hopeless?

19. During the last two weeks, on how many days have you had trouble concentrating or making decisions?

20. Does the individual have the ability to make decisions independently?

21. Does the individual appear to have short-term memory impairment?

Each one of these questions carries a score between 0 and 3. 0 indicates that there is no impairment, 1 is mild impairment, 2 is severe impairment, and 3 is total impairment. The next part of the test is used to determine who is going to help with services and how much time will be paid for by Medicaid. If the time exceeds the 8-hour per day limit, then your mother will not be allowed to get assistance at home; instead, Medicaid will encourage her to go to a facility. If you are insistent that your mother stay home, you will be responsible for taking on more responsibility. You want to be very careful signing up for this type of commitment as failure to provide services which you tell the government you will in fact offer as far as your mother's care goes, can be seen as a form of elderly neglect. This consequently, is considered a crime in the state of Texas. Your attorney has a legal obligation to report any abuse, exploitation or neglect of an elderly person, even if it violates attorney client privilege.

These programs may be able to assist her in cleaning and other housekeeping tasks. Also, they could provide for personal care services. In order for your mother to qualify, her income cannot exceed $2,205.00 per month. Another significant limitation to this program is that your mother cannot become eligible by using a "Qualified Income Trust" to reduce her income. The asset requirements are different under the Community Attendant Services and Family Care.

Community Attendant Services is the same as Medicaid ($3,00 for a couple and $2,000 for an individual). However, the Family Care program allows you to have up to $5,000 and $6,000 if you are married. If your mother wants to get on this particular program, we can execute the gifting strategy without the "transfer penalty." With this program, you do get to keep your income, but you have to spend her money every month or she will be disqualified from the program.

WARNING: IF YOUR MOTHER NEEDS TO GO INTO A NURSING HOME AFTER GIFTING IS MADE, THE TRANSFER PENALTY WILL APPLY.

Medicaid Funded Waiver Programs

These programs are referred to as "waiver" program because they waive the requirement of residing in a nursing home or ICF-IID facility. Home and Community-Based Services ("HCBS") beneficiaries will receive the same benefits as those on Medicaid Long-term care living in a nursing home. If your mother is eligible for both Medicaid and Medicare, she is considered "dual-eligible."

"Star+Plus Waiver" is probably the most likely program which your mother will use if she opts to stay at home. Since this program is funded by Medicaid, the eligibility requirements are the same as for nursing home care. A key difference between this program and the one above is that the transfer rule applies, but you can use a "Qualified Income Trust" if your mother's income is too high.

If your mother uses a Qualified Income Trust, any money above the income limit (as of 2018 it was $2,205) will have to serve as a copayment for the home care services. Unlike using the Client Needs Assessment test above, eligibility for this program is determined based upon whether or not your mother's needs can be met for not more than twice the cost of nursing home care.

Your mother can use this program to fund assisted living costs if she does not want to stay home, but also doesn't want to go into a nursing home. Bear in mind however, that this program does have an extensive waiting list ("interest list"). If the program is used to help with assisted living costs, your mother will need to give her income to the assisted living facility. She will be able to keep $85 ($25 more than a nursing home) for her personal care. If you believe your mother will be going to an assisted living facility in the future, it is important that you call Texas Health & Human Services Commission (512-424-6500) and get her placed on a waiting list today.

How to Bypass the Interest List

If your mother wants to stay home but needs immediate assistance, one strategy you can do is to have mom move into a facility. Once she has been approved for the Star+Plus Waiver services, she can then return home and still receive benefits.[10] This is known as the "Money Follows the Person" rule. It does not apply though if your mother fails to get approved for these services. Therefore, you have to make sure she is approved first, prior to moving her. It also stands to note here that future funding for this particular program is not guaranteed. Please reference the Star+Plus Handbook 3511-3526 to see the procedure for this rule.

OTHER HOUSING OPTIONS

The Housing Choice Voucher Program (Section 8)

If your mother is renting a residence that is not owned by a family member, Public Housing Authority (PHA) could be an option for getting the services needed to apply for assistance with rent payments. Some PHA's allow participants to use section 8 vouchers on their own mortgage payments. You

---

[10] Star+Plus Handbook 3510

would have to contact your local PHA to see if they offer this program. There is going to be a waiting list, but if your mother is homeless (living with you or another family member), in substandard housing, or paying more than 50% of her income towards rent, then she could be moved forward on this list. The program does not pay the full rent but does remit partial payment by way of a voucher. In limited situations, a family member can be a landlord, but your mother would have to be disabled and only the family member can provide the accommodations necessary. Here are the following points you should be aware of:

1.   The PHA will approve an application; they do not locate a residence. It will be your responsibility to find your mother a residence for which she will pay a reasonable rate. This residence will be inspected by the PHA. The landlord will also have to enter into an agreement with PHA.

2.   There are three eligibility requirements for your mother: (1) she must meet the definition of a family, (2) fall within the household income limits established by HUD (not the Medicaid income limit), and (3) be a U.S. citizen or eligible alien.

3.   The family definition is used to determine the household income requirement. The PHA in your area will have its own guidelines.

4.   If you would like to know the income limit for your area, you can go to www.huduser.org. The direct link, as of the writing of this book, is https://www.huduser.gov/portal/datasets/il.html. However, the link has been subject to change, so you might need to search on huduser.org.

5.   Your mother's social security check will be considered income, as will any income she receives from her retirement accounts. If

your mother is married and her spouse is in a nursing home, your mother's spouse's income is not counted as her income.

6.   If your mother has more than $5,000 in countable assets, a calculation will be done to determine how much those assets would contribute to her income if invested in a savings account, or of course, if there is actual income generated by the assets. They will use the higher of the two to determine income.

7.   The last issue which you should be aware of is the transfer rule. Assets which were transferred within the past two years will be considered an asset as far as the calculation of income. Your mother may choose to do a self-settled special needs trust and transfer her money into that trust with no penalty. However, the State of Texas would be the primary beneficiary of that trust.

Assisted Living Facilities

Assisted living facilities are not covered by Medicaid long-term care but can be covered by the Waiver program under Medicaid if they are certified to provide services under the Community Based Alternative Program ("Star+Plus Waiver"). The State of Texas maintains a site of all the assisted living facilities which are under the five waiver programs: https://apps.hhs.texas.gov/LTCSearch/.

There are three types of assisted living facilities:

1.   Type A are facilities whose residents do not require assistance during nighttime sleeping hours and are able to follow directions in emergency situations.

2.   Type B are facilities whose residents would need assistance in an emergency situation and who need some nighttime care.

3.   Type C are facilities which are a four-bed facility and meet the requirements for adult foster care.

4.   Unlicensed facilities are facilities which have four or fewer residences; these are generally created for those with less than $2,000 a month and who don't meet the medical necessity requirement to be in a nursing home.

OTHER GROUP LIVING ARRANGEMENTS

Board and Care Homes (Personal Care Homes)

These are homes with fewer than four residents who live together to cut down on costs. They are not per se illegal or bad. In fact, in some situations they could be a great option for your mother. In general, these types of places tend not to have a diversity of functions. However, in some situations these facilities can be better than a licensed assisted living facility. Usually, the cost will reflect the type of care you receive. These facilities are also known as adult care facilities, adult foster care homes, and residential care facilities. It is important to note that these are not licensed assisted living facilities, and some are being run illegally within the state. You need to investigate such accommodations very thoroughly prior to moving your mom into one.

Continuing Care Retirement Community

Your mother might want to spend her money on a larger facility which could take care of her for some time. These communities are designed for individuals who have the money to pay; these are not for those using government-based assistance programs. There have been problems seen with these types of places, as they can be quite expensive and also can go bankrupt down the road. Choosing such a facility is a rather difficult decision to make; most people cannot afford to stay in them for the remainder of their life and thus other arrangements would have to be made.

CHAPTER 4: THE NURSING HOME

T his book will go into deeper detail in just a bit regarding gifting rules and transfer penalty rules involved with Medicaid and asset transfers. Another issue, which I want to touch upon, and which many attorneys and people do not take into consideration, is the effect that the transferring of assets has on the nursing home. Let's say for instance that your mother gives away her property to the detriment of a nursing home, that nursing home could actually seek action against you: conspiracy to transfer assets.

The Nursing Home Agreement

A central issue in dealing with a nursing home is the nursing home agreement. Unfortunately, clients usually come to see me after they've already situated their parent or loved one in a nursing care facility and are not as informed as they should be in regard to the content of said agreement. When a family member places their loved one in a nursing home they don't necessarily take the time that they should in reading the contract or, for that matter, truly understanding whether or not they are guaranteeing their loved one's care. The Federal Nursing Home Reform Act (NHRA) does not allow a skilled nursing home to require you to guarantee payment in order for your mother to be admitted.

However, keep in mind that while the law states that a nursing home can't require an individual to guarantee payment for a person to be admitted, courts have held in certain situations that a third-party guarantor can be liable. The following are situations in which a court held a third party liable. Consider these the cautionary "don'ts" when dealing with a nursing home agreement.

1. **Don't Agree to Help Qualify for Medicaid**. A son, who held a power of attorney, signed as an agent but told the nursing home that he would assist them in getting mom qualified for Medicaid by spending down her money. He did not do what he had orally agreed to do, and the Court held that they had an oral contract; the son was thus liable for the payments[11].

2. **Don't Withhold Income from a Nursing Home.** An agent of a power of attorney withheld the monthly income of the resident[12]. You can be held personally liable for withholding monthly income from a nursing facility.

3. **Don't Sign as a "Responsible Party."** An agent signed as a responsible party and because of her actions, the mother ended up not being eligible for Medicaid[13].

---

[11] Glastonbury Healthcare Center, Inc. v. Esposito, 45 Conn. L. Rptr. 671, 2008 WL 2797003 (Conn. Super. Ct. 2008), opinion corrected, 2008 WL 4307883 (Conn. Super. Ct. 2008).

[12] Concord Health Care, Inc. V. Schroeder, 177 Ohio App. 3d 228, 2008-Ohio-3992, 894 N.E. 2d 351 (11th Dist. Trumbull County 2008).

[13] Sunrise Healthcare Corp. v. Azarigian, 76 Conn. App. 800, 821 A.2d 835 (2003)

4. **Don't Sign a Promissory Note**. Mom was Medicaid eligible when she went into the nursing home. She became ineligible for a period of time. The home incurred $13,000; the son subsequently signed a promissory note for that amount in his capacity as a power of attorney. Ultimately, the mother's estate was liable for the cost[14].

When it comes to assisting your mother with a nursing home or assisted living facility, the protocol is pretty simple: Do not lie to the nursing home. Disclose everything. In addition, sign only as a power of attorney and never as a responsible party. Also, do not withhold your mother's assets from the facility if they are not getting paid. If you are ever concerned that you do not understand what to do, most definitely consult with an Elder Law attorney.

Three Month Private-Pay Strategy

Most nursing homes give residents who are still living in their home preference for a Medicaid bed. Therefore, it usually is better to move into a nursing home as a private-pay resident. In Texas, a nursing home may obtain an additional Medicaid bed if they have a resident who has lived at the facility for at least three consecutive months (this does not include hospitalization).

---

[14] Pioneer Ridge Nursing Facility Operations, L.L.C. v. Emery, 41 Kan. App. 2d 414, 203 P.3d 4 (2009)

If you do intend to qualify for Medicaid, be sure to notify the business office at the nursing home of your choice, explain that you need to have a Medicaid bed allocated to you, and ask what, if any, wait is involved. Usually, you don't actually have to move to a different physical bed, but rather you need to be identified in the facility's records as one of a limited number of residents "in a Medicaid bed."

Eviction from Nursing Home

If your mother was to run out of money while at the nursing home, the facility may transfer her to another facility or even discharge her under certain situations. The following are reasons under the Nursing Facility Requirements for Licensure and Medicaid Certification (NFRLMC) section 19.502 why a nursing home may discharge or transfer your mother:

1. the transfer or discharge is necessary for your mother's welfare, and the resident's needs cannot be met in the facility;
2. the transfer or discharge is appropriate because your mother's health has improved sufficiently so that she no longer needs the services provided by the facility;
3. the safety of individuals in the facility is endangered;
4. the health of other individuals in the facility would otherwise be endangered;
5. your mother has failed, after reasonable and appropriate notice, to pay for (or to have paid under Medicare or Medicaid) a stay at the

facility. If your mother becomes eligible for Medicaid after admission to a facility, the facility may charge your mother only allowable charges under Medicaid;

6. your mother, responsible party, or family or legal representative requests a voluntary transfer or discharge; or

7. the facility ceases to operate as a nursing facility and no longer provides resident care.

If your mother was to be discharged or transferred, they would have to follow certain procedures:

1. The facility can't discharge your mother if she is waiting to get on Medicaid. If the facility provided your mother or you notice that they do not accept Medicaid, this rule does not apply. However, if they have Medicaid beds, then they can't discharge your mother. But, they could transfer her to another Medicaid facility.

2. The nursing home must give you or your mother 30-day notice of their plan and reason for the transfer or discharge. Of course, this time does not need to be given if it is an emergency. However, the nursing home has to keep records as to why it was an emergency to transfer or discharge your mother.

3. If the nursing home were to attempt to move your mother, they would have to do it in an orderly and safe manner.

4. If the nursing home were to transfer your mother to the hospital, they would need to provide you with their notice of bed-hold and readmission requirements.

5. The nursing home must have procedures for filing a complaint or grievance.

6. You can also appeal a transfer or discharge to a fair hearing board.

PART TWO: INCOME & RESOURCE REQUIREMENTS

CHAPTER 5: MEDICAID STATED INCOME REQUIREMENTS

As of January 1st 2018, your mother can qualify for Medicaid if she makes less than $2,205 a month. Many people mistakenly assume that the amount their mom receives every month constitutes the total amount of social security that gets factored into the income calculation. You have to remember that the Social Security Administration usually withholds taxes and premium payments; these actually need to be added back into the calculation for income. Upon taking everything into consideration, if your mother makes more than the income limit, she is disqualified from Medicaid benefits unless she has a Qualified Income Trust.

Remember: The Qualified Income Trust works for Medicaid based benefits. It does not work for Title 20 (block-grant) benefits.

Your mother's countable income is calculated by taking all of her income, any property or service she receives to meet basic food and shelter needs, minus exemptions and exclusions. Sometimes people will confuse the income rules for Medicaid with those that are put out by the IRS. The definition for income is a bit different when it comes to Medicaid. For example, helping pay for your mother to eat is not considered income to the IRS but it is income for Medicaid purposes.

If your mother is married, her spouse's income is not included as her income. The rule that Texas follows in determining whose income is who's is the "name on the check" rule. The name on the check rule simply means that income will be attributed to the person whose name is on the check. For example, if your mother receives an annuity payment in her name, it is her income not the income of both her and her spouse. If both your mother and her spouse are in the same nursing home, you double the stated income limit to determine the amount needed to qualify for Medicaid.

The following is a list of potential income sources and how they are treated:

1. VA reimbursements for unusual medical expenses, VA aid-and-attendance allowances, and VA house-bound allowances are not included as income for either applied income purposes or Medicaid eligibility.

2. Dividends could be considered income if they are received quarterly based upon an agreement. If dividends are irregular and not reasonably expected, then they can be excluded from income.

3. A Reverse Mortgage is not considered income for Medicaid. It is a reimbursement on a loan.

4. Royalty Income is treated as income, but you can make deductions for expenses as pertains to production and certain taxes.

5. Rental Income is income minus actual expenses which are allowed by the IRS less depreciation and depletion. Later we will go over rental strategies for primary residences.

If your mother is receiving Medicaid benefits and lives in a nursing home, all of her income, except for $60 (which she is allowed to keep for personal care), insurance premiums, and your mother's Medicare premium, will be paid to the nursing home. In return, Medicaid will pay the nursing home bill and all other expenses so covered under Medicaid. Medicaid wants your mother to continue to pay any insurance premiums which will assist in the cost of her care. Later in this book, we will go over another strategy where Medicaid allows your mother to keep up to $721 per month for her personal residence if your mother is likely to return home within six months of entry into a nursing facility or hospital.

Remember: if your mother is not in a nursing home and receives a home care program benefit, your mother may keep her income to pay for her expenses, but she will need to spend it.

The Income Tax Medical Deduction

If your mother meets the following requirements, all of her expenses for long-term care are deductible from taxable income as medical expenses. For this to apply, your mother must be a "chronically ill individual," and (2) the care must be provided pursuant to a plan of care.

At the time of writing this book, the author is unfamiliar with the changes that the new tax law has made to this particular deduction. A CPA or other licensed tax preparer should be able to assist you in determining whether your mother is a "chronically ill individual."

While changing tax laws could significantly impact this deduction, it is still a very important and often-overlooked one. Even if your mother did not take it in previous tax years, she can claim a refund for the last three tax years by filing form 1040X.

CHAPTER 6: QUALIFIED INCOME TRUST

Your mother is disqualified for Medicaid benefits if her income exceeds $2,205 a month (as of January 1st, 2018). This creates a definite problem because the cost of nursing home care is far more than $2,205 a month. In 1993, Congress addressed this by passing the Omnibus Budget Reconciliation Act which provided relief as it allows a person to transfer income into a trust to qualify for Medicaid benefits. As is the case with much of the information you find online, you might encounter conflicting information about this trust. In Texas, as well as in 12 other states, there is an income cap. Always remember that when you do read information on the internet regarding income requirements and options, each state has its own Medicaid program and therefore might not be the same.

A common question that I am asked is why the Qualified Income Trust (QIT) does not work for some programs but does for others. Fortunately, there is an easy answer. The Omnibus Budget Reconciliation Act only applies to Medicaid nursing home care programs or programs which have been specifically affected by this act. It does not however apply to Title 20 (Block-Grant) which cover programs like Community Care that assist with home services.

Your mother's Qualified Income Trust is funded by all of her available income like social security, pensions, or any other income that comes at least on a quarterly basis or has a contractual arrangement for payment. If income accumulates in your mother's trust, upon her death it will be paid to the Texas Health and Human Services Commission as reimbursement to the Texas Medicaid Program for benefits provided. You do not need to obtain a tax identification number for the trust. You should use your mother's social security number.

If you deposit any VA benefits into a QIT, it will be considered income to your mother. However, there is little to no benefit in not putting this into the trust

How to Open a Checking Account

After your mother's trust agreement has been executed and if your mother then plans to apply for Medicaid benefits, a checking account will need to be opened in the name of the trust. The trust account must contain only your mother's income. Often, I create a QIT with the anticipation that my client is going to go on Medicaid. If however, your mother is not going into a facility anytime soon, then do not open a checking account in the name of the trust.

Banks will generally require a deposit when you do go in to open the Trust checking account. A small amount of your mother's or another party's assets may be used to fund the opening of such an account. Only deposit your mother's income after the account is opened. Any additional amounts will be considered a gift to your mother.

Directing all of your mother's income to the trust will simplify having to transfer it every month. If you are unable to direct the income because a source refuses to do so, then you may transfer her income from the current account to the trust account. It's important that your mother's income is transferred to the trust checking account in the month that it is received. You can set this up by opting for automatic transfer within the online banking platform. <u>DO NOT TRANSFER OTHER ASSETS TO THE TRUST</u>.

You may use an existing account as the QIT trust account if you: (1) reduce the account to zero before switching it over, (2) remove all other people on the account, and (3) have the Trust instrument reflect ownership of the account.

Distributions from the Trust

The following distributions need to be made by the Trustee from the trust on a monthly basis:

1.   Personal Needs Allowance: This money is for your mother to use for her personal needs. Medicaid updates the personal needs allowance every few years. In Texas, it is currently $60 a month. You should review the law to see if the amount increases so your mother can purchase more items she may need. Remember that your mother should not save too much money because she could accidently disqualify herself from Medicaid if she retains too much money.

2.   **Spousal Maintenance:** If your mother is married, her spouse has a right to a monthly maintenance needs allowance (this amount changes yearly).

3.   **Nursing Home Payment:** The Trustee must pay the nursing home the remaining amount.

There should not be any funds remaining in the account at the end of the month. If funds do remain in the checking account, they must be retained in the trust and will be paid to the State of Texas upon your mother's death.

Keep in mind that you will need to reconcile the trust's checking account each month; be sure to save all canceled checks, deposit tickets, and bank statements. You can't use your mother's income to hire someone to do this. You should not need to file a tax return for this trust because it should not make more than $100 during the year.

CHAPTER 7: INCOME SHIFTING STRATEGIES

Income is determined by the 'name on the check' rule. As previously mentioned, this means that whomever the check is made payable to, is the owner of that check and thus that income. Often a pension is either in the name of your mother or her spouse. Shifting the income from the institutionalized spouse to the spouse living outside a nursing home can be done through a Qualified Domestic Relation Order (QDRO).

The process for doing this is as follows:

1. Make sure that you get a Qualified Income Trust because this strategy often takes a few months to process.
2. Your mother will not need to file for divorce in order to shift the income.
3. Both your mother and her spouse will need to be represented by counsel as this is litigation.
4. Your attorney will need to contact the pension administrator to make sure that the requirements of I.R.C. section 414(p) are met before the order is presented to the judge.
5. It should be an uncontested matter which means you should be able to have an uncontested hearing.

Annuity Income Strategy

If your mother is married she could convert an asset to income if it is over the spousal protected resource amount (SPRA). This strategy requires purchasing an irrevocable single-premium annuity for no greater than the life expectancy of the non-institutionalized spouse. For example, your mother and her spouse have $250,000 over the spousal protected resource amount. If they were to purchase an irrevocable single-premium annuity for the proper time frame in the name of the spouse who is not living in a nursing home and doesn't need care in the foreseeable future, this income would be paid to the non-institutionalized spouse (the spouse not in the nursing home) and the $250,000 would no longer be considered an asset. The income would not be counted either because the name on the check would be the non-institutionalized spouse and therefore be considered his or her money.

CHAPTER 8: RESOURCE REQUIREMENTS

A s you are aware, if your mother has too many resources she is not eligible for Medicaid benefits. Resources are defined as: "cash, other liquid assets, or any real or personal property or other non-liquid assets owned by a client, his spouse, or parent that could be converted to cash.[15]" One incredibly important rule to understand is when exactly resources are counted; they are counted at 12:01 a.m. on the first day of the month. At some point during the month your mother may have more than the resource limits (see those listed below); however, by the end of the month, the assets must be spent down so that they fall under the countable resource limit. The following are the resource limits based upon family structure:

1. If your mother is unmarried, the countable resource limit is $2,000.
2. If your mother is married with a spouse who is also eligible for Medicaid, the countable resource limit is $3,000.
3. If your mother is married with an ineligible (not eligible for Medicaid benefits) spouse, then it is half of the couple's combined resources, subject to a minimum "spousal protected resource amount" (SPRA) of $24,720 (in 2018) and a maximum resource standard of $123,600. The SPRA can be expanded depending upon

---

[15] MEPD section E-3310

some strategies which might be employed—discussed later in this book under "Medicaid Spousal Impoverishment" rules.

4. Now to complicate matters further, if your mother and her spouse both reside in a nursing facility and only one of them applies for Medicaid, then the countable resource limit is $2,000. The resources of the spouse who did not apply are not resources of the spouse who applied because they are not in the same household.

Another important rule to understand is that a resource is only considered countable if it is (1) owned by your mother, and (2) your mother has to have the "right, authority, or power to liquidate the property or her share of it.[16]" From time to time it will happen that a child and parent have a joint bank account, with the assets in said account belonging to the child. In this situation you can file a *Medicaid Form H1299, Request for Joint Bank Account Information*, which will allow you to prove true ownership of the funds. An irrevocable trust is another way that resources could be transferred out of your estate. The trust cannot distribute any money to your mother in any way. Transfers to this trust will be subject to the penalty period.

It is possible your mother might be unaware of property that she owns. Especially if mental capacity issues are involved, coming across previously unknown property is not unheard of. If you were to discover that your

---

[16] MEPD section F-1311

mother has property not disclosed to Medicaid like a plot of land, it will be considered income in the month that it is discovered and converted to a resource on the first day of the next month. Certain assets will be given a longer period of time to be counted as a resource. For example, burial expenses will have to be spent within two months and proceeds from property and casualty insurance must be spent within nine months.

CHAPTER 9: MEDICAID SPOUSAL IMPOVERISHMENT RULE

Before September 30th, 1989, elderly couples were often forced to divorce because there were little to no protections for a community spouse who remained at home while the other was receiving Medicaid benefits in a nursing home. However, the federal government has since provided a way for a spouse who remains home to be able to retain enough resources to provide for his or her care.

In order for the spousal impoverishment rule to apply, either your mother or her spouse must be: (1) in a medical institution or nursing facility, (2) reside there for at least 30 days, while the other spouse does not reside in a medical institution. Sometimes determining whether or not the non-institutional spouse (sometimes referred to as the "community spouse") resides in a medical institution can be tricky. For example, if the community spouse resides in an assisted living facility, Medicaid may consider him or her to be "in the community" meaning he/she is not institutionalized.

In order for you to determine whether your mother can shelter more than the spousal protected resource amount (SPRA) of $24,720 (in 2018) and a maximum resource standard of $123,600, the above eligibility rule must apply, and we also need to do the following calculation. For the calculation below, I'm going to assume that your mother's spouse is institutionalized, and your mother is the community spouse.

1. Determine the "snapshot date". This is done by finding the date your mother's spouse became institutionalized and then adding on thirty days. The snapshot date is on the next first day of the month. For example, Jim is institutionalized on August 5th, 2018. He continues to remain in a facility and on September 4th, 2018 he has been institutionalized for 30 days. So, October 1st, 2018 at 12:01 a.m. is the snapshot date. Form 1272 is where you fill out the snapshot date.

2. SPRA is calculated by taking the greater of (1) one-half of your mother and her spouse's combined countable resources, not to exceed $123,600 (in 2018) or (2) taking the minimum of $24,720.

3. If your mother's income and her spouse's income is less than the "minimum monthly maintenance needs allowance" (MMMNA and yes, this is the actual name) of $3,090, then she can seek additional resources to exclude. The following is the calculation used to determine the expanded SPRA:

Calculation	Example
Add up your mother and her spouse's monthly income (income from a countable resource is not included).	$750 +1,150 = $1,900
Subtract $60 personal needs allowance.	$1,900 - 60 = $1,840

Subtract the MMMNA ($3,090 in 2018) from your mother's income.	$1,900 - $3,090 = $1,190
This is the "shortfall" amount	$1,190
Multiply the shortfall amount by 12 to get the "annual shortfall amount."	$14,280
Divide your mother's annual shortfall amount by the one-year certificate deposit rate.	$14,280/.025 = $571,200

The expanded SPRA cannot exceed your mother and her spouse's combined countable resources. In other words, in the above example, if your mother and her spouse only have assets of $200,000, then $200,000 is the max amount that can be protected. If they had $700,000, then they could protect up to $571,200.

SPRA Community Spouse Transfer Strategy

This may be a strategy which can be used by your mother if she qualifies; find out if the SPRA applies to your mother. If we follow the previous example and are able to protect a certain resource, we can implement the following strategy:

1. Have your mother and her spouse enter into a marital property agreement transferring all the assets to your mother (as long as your

mother is not the institutionalized spouse). Your mother's spouse can transfer real estate only through a deed. It is important that the deed contain language signifying that the property is currently community property and it is now becoming separate property.

2. Your mother can choose who she wants to leave her property to through the execution of a will, trust, or other testamentary document. However, most individuals wish to leave their property to their spouse. If this is your mom's desire, she can execute a will leaving her property to a trust for the benefit of her spouse. The key provision here is that the trustee cannot be her spouse and cannot have any discretion of the assets of the trust. As long as the trust is created correctly, then the assets in the trust are not considered a resource of her spouse and he will be able to keep Medicaid benefits. Lastly, the alternate beneficiaries may be the children.

The key provisions of this strategy are that we have been able to protect some resources through SPRA or expanded SPRA. Federal law states, "no resources of the community spouse (your mother in this example) shall be deemed available to the institutionalized spouse.[17]" Also, your mother can transfer the assets without her spouse being subject to the gifting penalty.

---

[17] 42 U.S.C.A. section 1396r-5(e)(2)(B);

PART THREE: MEDICAID STRATEGIES

CHAPTER 10: SPEND DOWN STRATEGY

One way to hasten your mother's eligibility for Medicaid is to spend her countable resources to get her qualified for Medicaid. Here are some things you can spend your mother's assets on in order for her to qualify for Medicaid:

1. **Dream Vacation.** Many people live paycheck to paycheck for their entire lives. Maybe your mother has always wanted to visit Alaska; she may not get another chance to do so. If your mother has a dream vacation in mind, try to convince her to go. This really is her last opportunity.

2. **Purchase of Needed Services.** As an attorney, this is my favorite strategy. She can use her money to pay for services which she needs. For example, attorney's fees, medical needs, dental bills, and other fees.

3. **Equipment Needed**. A nursing home can be a difficult place in which to live at times. From personal experience, I know that my aunt experienced down times during which the family purchased items such as coloring books to keep her entertained. Your mother may even want to purchase a TV, iPad or some such similar device.

4. **Pay Debts.** For some people, paying off any debts they may have accrued constitutes a moral or religious obligation. Please make sure your mother understands this is her last opportunity to pay her debts.

5. **Purchase Exempt Resources with Countable Resources.** Your mother could purchase exempt assets as a method to reduce her countable resources. Here are a few examples:

   a. A personal residence to which your mother intends to return, up to a maximum equity value of $543,000;

   b. Repairs or improvements on her home;

   c. Pay down on a mortgage;

   d. One vehicle, keeping in mind that your mother has to be able to use it for transportation;

   e. Cash Value Life insurance with a death benefit and cash value of not more than $1,500;

   f. Term life insurance with an unlimited death benefit. This is a tricky rule, so you need to talk to your attorney;

   g. Burial plots. Your mother can purchase one for herself, her spouse, her children, her brothers or sisters, her parents. A "burial space" includes a grave site, burial plot, crypt, mausoleum, casket, urn, niche or other repository;

   h. Certain trade or business property and other property essential to self-support (not including liquid resources, except cash used in a trade or business);

   i. Burial funds with a maximum value of $1,500; or a prepaid, irrevocable funeral contract for the applicant, with no limit as to value. You can shelter the entire cost of any funeral contract if it is nonrefundable;

j. Household goods and personal effects if they are not for investment purposes. No gold coins or jewelry. Medical equipment is exempt;

k. Prepayments to the nursing home. This rule allows that the amount prepaid to the nursing home can only be refunded to your mother after Medicaid pays retroactively for the months for which your mother already paid privately.

CHAPTER 11: SELF-SETTLED TRUST STRATEGIES

The Pooled Self-Settled Trust

A self-settled pooled supplemental needs trust is a trust which your mother funds but is managed by a non-profit. Usually, these types of trusts have reduced costs which allow them to be more efficient. Each trust has a sub-account maintained and invested by the non-profit. The account can only be used for the benefit of your mother. If your mother is 65 or older, then the transfer penalty will apply to any transfers not for your mother's benefit. For example, if money is transferred to a self-settled pooled supplemental needs trust and some of the money is used to purchase a plane ticket for a daughter, then the amount used to purchase a plane ticket will be subject to the transfer penalty.

The State of Texas will be the primary beneficiary of the trust upon your mother's death. Certain pooled trusts have already been set up and approved by HHSC in Texas. The ARC of Texas operates different trusts and these can be established without the services of an attorney.

The Under 65 Special Needs Trust Strategy

If your mother has NOT attained the age of 65 and is disabled, she can transfer all of her money into a self-settled special needs trust for her benefit. Assets cannot be added after she reaches the age of 65. This trust will have to be irrevocable and established by a parent, grandparent, legal guardian, or a court. The State of Texas will be the beneficiary of this trust upon the death of your mother.

The trust can make distributions for your mother's benefit. The following are ways to distribute the money so that it is not considered income. The trust can make payments directly to providers of anything other than food or shelter. The following are allowed payments:

1. personal services;
2. medical expenses not paid by public benefits or insurance;
3. vehicle and transportation expenses;
4. entertainment expenses;
5. educational expenses.

If your mother is on a Community Based Alternative program, then payments for food or shelter do not count as "income." If she is on a Community Care program, then distribution for shelter and food are considered income.

CHAPTER 12: GIFTING STRATEGY

Your mother cannot just give you all of her assets and thereby qualify for Medicaid. Most people have heard that it is against the law to transfer someone's assets to qualify for Medicaid long-term care. In actuality, the rule states that a person can transfer assets for less than fair market value, but will ultimately be subject to a transfer penalty. This penalty exists because otherwise, if there were no penalty, then a person could simply wait until he or she was about to enter a facility and subsequently transfer all assets to his or her loved ones.

Sometimes there is confusion regarding debtor-creditor or bankruptcy laws and those applicable to Medicaid benefits. A "fraudulent transfer" for bankruptcy purposes also has a 5-year look back penalty, but its application is vastly different from that of Medicaid gifting rules. In addition to the confusion between bankruptcy transfer rules and Medicaid laws, many of my clients also confuse federal gift tax rules. For example, a person can transfer up to $15,000 a year without having to report it to the IRS as a gift. Whereas when it comes to Medicaid, *any* amount given has to be reported; do not confuse federal gift tax rules with the Medicaid gifting rules.

Unless an exception applies, any assets, funds or property your mother or her spouse transfers for less than fair market value will result in ineligibility as far as qualifying for Medicaid benefits. To be exact, the period of time your mother will be ineligible for Medicaid is one day for every $172.65

she gives away. The period of ineligibility applies only to those gifts which are given during the "lookback period." Currently, the lookback period applies to the previous 60 months before the calendar month in which the Medicaid application is filed. All transfers which are made during this time are thus presumed to be a gift given in order for your mom to qualify for Medicaid. The burden therefore falls upon your mother to show that an exception applies.

While the lookback period is 60 months, the ineligibility period does not begin until your mother is in a nursing home and otherwise meets all the requirements for Medicaid eligibility. It is important to understand exactly when the penalty period will begin. Under the federal statute, Medicaid eligibility begins, "the date on which the individual is eligible for medical assistance under the State plan and would otherwise be receiving institutional level care..."[18]. It is important to note that gifts cannot be given with the intent to qualify for Medicaid. This is why if your mother will be needing long-term care soon, a gifting strategy is probably not a good option. Gifts of $200 within a calendar month are usually considered too small to be included in the transfer penalty.

The following example can better help put gifting and the transfer penalty into perspective:

---

[18] 42 U.S.C. section 1396p(c)(1)(D)(ii); Medicaid for the Elderly and People with Disabilities Handbook section I-5200.

Your mother decides to give you $100,000. She gifted this amount to you on August 4th, 2018. Your mother then proceeds to go into a nursing facility on November 20th, 2020. She applies for Medicaid on that date and is eligible; this is when the penalty kicks in. The penalty would be $100,000 divided by $172.65 for a total of 579 days. Your mother would thus be barred from Medicaid Benefits until June 22, 2022.

Given the severity of the penalty incurred, you can easily see that gifting property to anyone other than a community spouse for SPRA is usually not a good strategy. Gifting your money means you will be giving up control and it must be absolute and irrevocable.

A number of parents plan to gift their property to their children and then wait out the 60-month lookback period before applying for Medicaid. There are problems inherent with this particular strategy as well. First of all, the person to whom you gift could die, thereby leaving all of your mother's property, via a will or beneficiary designation, to someone who consequently runs off with the money. The money could also be taken by a spendthrift spouse. If the recipient has creditors, they could lay claim to the money; similarly, if they owe back taxes, the IRS could also take any available funds. Perhaps the person has a dire need and thus uses the money out of pure necessity. Finally, there is always the reality that the laws could change.

Exclusions from Gifting

Your mother can make the following transfers without a penalty. Tithing to your mother's church is not an exempt transfer; however, HHSC does not penalize these transfers as long as they end when the application is filed. The following are exclusions from the gifting rule:

1. Gifts to minors. Your mother may place money into a Uniform Transfer to Minors Act (UTMA account for the benefit of someone under 21 years of age or another such irrevocable college savings plans).

2. Transferring a home. Your mother could transfer her interest in her home to:
   a. Her spouse;
   b. A child under the age of 21;
   c. A child of any age who meets the requirements of disability under SSA;
   d. Your mother's sibling who has an interest in the home and who has resided in the home for at least one year;
   e. Your mother's children who resided in the home for at least two years before your mother is institutionalized and the child who cared for your mother delayed institutionalization.

3. Transfers of guardians to avoid taxes.

4. Transfers to your mother's spouse.

5. Transfer to your mother's disabled child.

CHAPTER 13: ANNUITY STRATEGY

Another great planning strategy—under certain circumstances—could be the purchase of an annuity. However, this planning is complicated, and always remember that you cannot do this for the sole purpose of qualifying for Medicaid benefits. The following section is intended to help you understand the rules when it comes to purchasing an annuity for your mother or her spouse.

Annuity payments are usually considered income, not a resource, under the Texas Medicaid program. When applying for Medicaid, there are two general types of annuities allowed: (1) periodic payments for returns of prior services (commonly known as a pension); and (2) a contract or agreement for an amount to be paid at regular intervals.

Before the Deficit Reduction Act (DRA) of 2005, annuities were treated differently for Medicaid purposes. Since this book is being written in 2018, we will focus our attention on "post-DRA" annuities. The Texas Health & Human Services Commission divides annuities into: (1) employment-related, (2) retirement-related, and (3) all other annuities.

When an annuity meets the post-DRA terms and conditions:
1. The annuity will not count as a resource;
2. Transfers to the annuity are not considered a transfer of assets; and

3. The monthly payments are considered unearned income[19].

Employment-Related Annuity (ERA)

An ERA is an annuity that represents a return on prior services through an employer. Most people know this as a pension or a retirement plan which is payable on a monthly basis. This would include things such as Teacher Retirement, Ford Motor Pension, or Federal Employee Retirement System (FERS). An ERA is NEVER a resource no matter when it was created, but it is treated as income.

Retirement-Related Annuity (RRA)

An RRA is an annuity which was "purchased by or on behalf of an annuitant in an institutional setting.[20]" If your mother purchased the annuity before February 8th, 2006, then the annuity is not a resource and will be treated as income. If your mother purchases or plans to purchase an annuity after February 8th, 2006, then whether it is a resource or income is determined by the following rule.

1. If the RRA is described in subsection (b) or (q) of § 408 of the Internal Revenue Code of 1986. These are called the following:
   a. §408(b) is an Individual Retirement Annuity;
   b. §408(q) is a §457 Deferred Compensation Deemed IRA
2. If the RRA is purchased with proceeds from:
   a. §408(a) Traditional IRA

---

[19] MEPD F-7200 Post-Deficit Reduction Act (DRA) Treatment of an Annuity
[20] 1 Texas. Admin, Code § 358.333(a)(2)

b. §408(c)(p) SIMPLE IRA

c. §408(k) SEP-IRA

d. §408A ROTH IRA

By purchasing an annuity from one of these accounts, the annuity will not be considered a resource but any income from the annuity will be treated as income to your mother. In addition, the State of Texas does not need to be put on as the primary beneficiary of the annuity in order for it to qualify.

All Other Compliant Annuities (AOCA)

All other annuities can be broken down into two different types—those annuities purchased by a Medicaid applicant: (1) without a community spouse (remember: community spouse has a particular definition); (2) with a community spouse.

Without a Community Spouse

An AOCA purchased without a community spouse will be treated as a resource *unless* all of the following conditions are met:

1. It is in the name of your mother or her spouse, whichever person is institutionalized;
2. It provides for equal payments throughout the annuity;
3. It is irrevocable and non-assignable;
4. Does not have any balloon payments or deferral payments;

5. The principal investment needs to be guaranteed to return to the institutionalized spouse within his or her lifetime (use the Social Security Administration Online Period Life Table);

6. The State of Texas is the primary beneficiary for the total amount paid on behalf of the institutionalized individual.

With a Community Spouse

If your mother or her spouse is a community spouse, then the following rules need to be followed:

1. It is in the name of your mother or her spouse, whichever person is institutionalized;

2. It provides for equal payments throughout the annuity;

3. It is irrevocable and non-assignable;

4. Does not have any balloon payments or deferral payments;

5. The principal investment needs to be guaranteed to return to the community spouse within his or her lifetime (use the Social Security Administration Online Period Life Table); and

6. The remainder beneficiary is different depending on who is the annuitant.

    a. Annuity pays **Institutional Spouse**: The primary beneficiary can be the community spouse, a minor, or a disabled child—as long as the State of Texas is the secondary beneficiary.

b. Annuity pays **Community Spouse**: The primary beneficiary can be a minor or a disabled child. However, if there are no minor children or disabled children, then the State of Texas must be the primary beneficiary for the total amount paid on behalf of the institutionalized individual.

All Other Non-Compliant Annuities

If your mother purchases an annuity that does not comply with the above criteria, then that annuity if revocable, is a countable asset valued at current fair market value. If it is irrevocable, then its purchase price is considered a transfer of assets, but it is not considered a countable asset.

IRA Annuities Planning

If your mother or her spouse has an IRA under the Texas Medicaid Program, annuities also include deferred annuities. As of 2018, an individual in Texas may take the assets in their IRA and purchase a deferred annuity (an annuity which does not pay out). This annuity will not be considered a transfer of assets or be considered a resource for Medicaid eligibility. The deferred status means that no income will be coming out of the annuity. Also, the State of Texas does not need to be the primary beneficiary. This is a strategy created because the law has thus far been undefined and will likely be changed in the future.

Pre-DRA Annuities

This book will not deal with Pre-DRA Annuities (because they are so rare). If your mother has a Pre-DRA annuity, then you should definitely contact an attorney to assist you in determining if it is in fact considered a resource.

CHAPTER 14: HALF LOAF STRATEGY

I f your mother is in a pinch, and we don't have time to do any sort of extensive planning, then the modern Half-a-Loaf strategy might work for her. The idea is that you transfer about 50 to 60% of countable assets to anyone your mother chooses and then purchase a Medicaid annuity to pay for medical expenses during the penalty period. Please note however, that if your mother no longer has the mental capacity to gift property, she might not be able to utilize this strategy.

As we discussed above, a Medicaid compliant annuity in the state of Texas is not considered a countable resource or a transfer of assets for Medicaid purposes. The amount which your mother gifts to her loved one will trigger the penalty period. The penalty period will not begin until the Medicaid Effective Date. This is the first day your mother enters the nursing home. To make the situation more complicated, in Texas, the end date will be the first full month in which she is penalty-free.

A properly designed plan is to have the Medicaid Annuity end when the penalty period ends. The income from the annuity will no longer be counted and as soon as the penalty period has passed, your mother will be eligible. You will need to purchase an annuity because your mother will need someone to pay for the time she is penalized, and the annuity is not considered a countable resource.

Here is an example of a modern Half-a-Loaf Strategy:

This was an actual situation one of my previous clients faced. Let's assume your mother had $460,200 left to her name. If your mother was paying $6,500.00 per month for her nursing home care, and her monthly income was $2,500.00, she would therefore have a monthly income shortfall of $4,000.00. With the monthly income shortfall being added to the Texas Monthly Divestment Penalty Divisor of $5,234.00, the total amount equals $9,234.00. This amount would then be divided into the spend-down amount of $460,200.00, the resulting figure equates to a 50.67 month penalty period.

If this was your mother's situation, the immediate gift amount will equal 50.67 times the Texas Monthly Divestment Penalty Divisor amount of $5,234.00, or $265,206.78.

Your mother's spend-down amount of $460,200.00 being reduced by the gift amount of $265,582.02, the Medicaid Compliant Annuity amount equals the difference, or $194,993.22.

Period Certain	Single Premium	Monthly Payout	Total Payout
50 Months	$194,993.22	$3,949.65	$197,482.50

During the 51-month annuity period certain, your mother will have a total monthly income of $6,449.65, which is then available to pay the nursing home. Given nursing home charges of $6,500.00 per month, less the total monthly income of $6,449.65, the monthly income shortfall amount equals the difference, or $50.35. Added up, over the course of the 51-month annuity period certain, the total income shortfall amounts to 3,506.59.

On the assumption that your mother retains $1,800.00 or less of countable resources, she would be in a position to cover the monthly income shortfall of $2,517.50 and the amount of $3,506.59 due to the nursing home, which comes to a complete shortfall of $6,024.09. As a result of this plan, we would be able to do the following:

1. Your mother's loved one will receive a gift of $265,206.78.
2. Immediately following the 50.67-month divestment penalty period, your mother will be eligible for Texas Medicaid benefits.
3. With your mother paying approximately $6,500.00 per month for her nursing home care, by qualifying for Texas Medicaid benefits, and with her Medicaid monthly co-pay being $2,440.00, she will experience a monthly savings of $4,060.00.
4. If your mother decided not to proceed with the Gifting/Medicaid Compliant Annuity Plan, and instead continues to privately pay for her nursing home care, she will exhaust her entire spend-down amount in approximately 115 months.
5. As you can see, this strategy if implemented correctly could save your mother hundreds of thousands of dollars.

CHAPTER 15: PRIMARY RESIDENCE STRATEGY

Your mother may protect a significant portion of her wealth by owning a home or purchasing a home, given the condition that she resides in that home for some period of time, and if she moves from the home, it has to be with the intent to return whenever she is able to do so. Medicaid will require her or you to sign a document to this effect.

I often have clients whose mother resides with them. Your mother can actually purchase an interest in your home. She does not need to own 100% of the house. In buying a portion of your home, she can thus shelter some of her money. This has to be done using the fair market value of the home. And in this way, we can calculate the proper payment for the home. Any taxes owed must be dealt with, and you also have to make sure that there are no liens on the property at time of purchase. In order to ensure that this strategy is executed correctly, I recommend that my clients use a title company to check that everything is in order. This generally adds about a 1% cost to the purchase.

If your mother purchases a life estate (a life estate is a property interest which gives someone the right to live in the home for the remainder of his or her life) in your home, then it will be considered a transfer of assets until she has resided in the home for one year.

While this strategy might sound good to some people, it can give rise to a few problematic issues down the road. For instance, if your mother does purchase an interest in your home, she may want her interest to go to her kids upon her passing. That potentially means that your siblings might have an ownership interest in your primary residence after your mother's death.

Another issue concerns your mother's right to partition the property. As people age, many times their personalities change significantly. While it may sound horrible, there could come a time when you do not want your mother to live with you any longer. In order to get your mother to move, you would actually have to buy her out of her interest in the home. This could certainly get costly. I often encourage people to put aside some money, regardless of your love for your mom, with the expectation that someday they will have to buy her out. There is also the possibility that you might want to move. However, this is not an issue if you are going to have your mother move with you.

Another complicating factor comes with determining exactly how much ownership interest your mother will receive upon purchasing the home. People frequently want to use tax appraisal values for this purpose. However, this assessment might not be accurate because the value of the house is more. Really, the only way to come to a fair purchase price is to contact a real estate agent and get comps on your home. If there is a mortgage on the property your mother is going to purchase, she must purchase an interest equal to your equity. So for example, if your home is worth $350,000 and you have a $300,000 mortgage, and it has been determined that your mother is going to give you $30,000 to purchase an interest in your home, you would need to divide $30,000 into $50,000 which gives you 60%.

And things can get much more complicated. Let's assume you only have $50,000 in equity and your mother pays you $100,000 to own the house. In this situation, your mother would become full owner of the property plus any additional amount would go to pay down the mortgage. None of the extra income could go to you outright.

Rental Income from Primary Residence

If your mother wants to rent her property while she is receiving Medicaid benefits, there are specific rules that need to be followed. If your mother intends to return home within six months, your mother may rent out the residence for the cost of taxes, insurance and other expenses to maintain it. That way the home is kept up, and there is not a need to pay net rent to the nursing home.

When your mother does not have an intent to return home in six months the plan to rent becomes a lot more difficult. If your mother has a mortgage and wants to rent out her property, the following rules provided by Texas Medicaid apply:

1. If your mother's homestead is *vacant* and a third party is making the person's mortgage payments using the person's own funds, these payments are *not income* to your mother.

2. If your mother's homestead is *rented* and the *lease agreement* specifies that the tenant pay the person's mortgage company in lieu of rent, these payments are countable income to your mother and are treated as *rental income.*

3. If your mother's homestead is *rented* and there is *no lease agreement*, voluntary payments of your mother's mortgage by the tenant directly to the mortgage company are considered to be a "gift" to your mother and are *countable income.*[21]

Sublease Strategy

If you plan to rent out your mother's home while she is in a nursing home and Medicaid is paying for her care, the strategy is a little complicated. The following are the points that will need to be followed:

1. If your mother is married, then the simplest strategy for keeping rental income is to have your mother transfer her ownership of the home to her spouse. This is done by having her draft a deed in favor of her spouse and disclaiming all ownership interest. This transfer is

---

[21] MEPD E-3342

not subject to the penalty because it is a transfer to a community spouse.

2. You will have to make the principal payments on the home. (If your mother is able, she will have to make the interest payments on the home.)

3. You will sublet the home to a person for just the principal payments, taxes, and other maintenance on the property.

4. You will not be able to make any profit. If you do make a profit, the Health and Human Service Commission will report you to Texas Adult Protective Services for exploitation.

5. If you do make a profit, you'll need to give it to the nursing home.

6. If your mother does not have a mortgage, just lease the property for the taxes, insurance and other expenses.

7. If that is not possible, you can enter into an escrow arrangement with a real estate agent who manages property. This is a difficult strategy which might require a court order so as not to allow distribution from the escrow account to your mother, and thereby prevent the assets from being counted as a resource to Medicaid.

Right to Pay Mortgage if Mom Can Return Home

If your mother has been admitted to a nursing home and a doctor provides a written statement that she is likely to return home within 6 months, your mother may use up to a total of $721 of her income to pay her mortgage or rent payment and utilities. If you are going to make this claim you must do it within 90 days of the date your mother enters the nursing home or the date she enters a hospital.

PART FOUR: MEDICAID ESTATE RECOVERY PROGRAM

CHAPTER 16: TEXAS MEDICAID ESTATE RECOVERY PROGRAM

The federal government requires that the State of Texas seek to recover funds from any individual who is receiving Medicaid Benefits.[22] In 2003, Texas enacted the Medicaid Estate Recovery Program (MERP) under the Department of Aging and Disability Services (DADS); Health Management Systems, Inc. (HMS) is contracted to collect MERP claims.

Medicaid can seek recovery from the estate of a deceased Medicaid recipient as long as that individual is 55 or older. The definition for estate is "real and personal property of the decedent, both as such property originally existed and as from time to time changed in form by sale, reinvestment, or otherwise, and as augmented by an accretions and additions and substitutions that are included in the definition of the probate estate found in the Texas Estate Code[23]." Under this definition, it has been deemed that property passing outside of probate is not subject to a MERP claim. While this is the law as of 2018, it could always change. Also, keep in mind that if a person filed an application before March 1st, 2005, he or she is "grandfathered," and the estate recovery provisions do not apply.

---

[22] 42 U.S.C.A. § 1396p
[23] Tex. Admin Code § 373.105(6)

MERP will initiate a claims procedure within thirty days after the death of a Medicaid recipient. Such a procedure begins when they file a document titled "Notice of Intent to File a Claim." It is important to know that if you intend to file an Undue Hardship Waiver Request or a request for deduction by documentation, you will need to do so within 60 days of the Notice of Intent to File Claim. If you miss this deadline or otherwise fail to file these applications, you can still negotiate down the claim. The last attempt you have to reduce the amount owed to MERP is to file claims within the probate court. In Texas, an MERP claim is a Class 7 claim. Many claims come before an MERP claim like attorney fees, funeral expenses and other costs. However, if a property is to be sold, a title company will want the MERP claim satisfied before it will close on the home.

The following people are exempt from a MERP claim:

1. Surviving Spouse;
2. Surviving child under the age of 21;
3. Surviving child of any age who is blind or disabled as defined by 42 U.S.C.A. §1382c; or
4. Unmarried adult child residing continuously in the decedent's homestead for at least one year prior to the time of the Medicaid recipient's death.

CHAPTER 17: LADY BIRD DEED VS. TRANFER ON DEATH DEED & BENEFICIARY DESIGNATION OF A MOTOR VEHICLE

An Enhanced Life Estate Deed or a "Lady Bird Deed" is a deed which, as far as her estate planning is concerned, can help your mom in primarily two ways: (1) avoiding probate by passing property to a beneficiary upon the death of the grantor, and (2) avoiding the Medicaid Estate Recovery Program of Texas. The "Lady Bird Deed" received its name from a fictional character illustrated by Jerome Ira Solkoff. In his example, he used United States President Lyndon Johnson's wife, Claudia Alta "Lady Bird" Johnson to show how an enhanced life estate deed would work for avoiding a Medicaid Lien in Florida. The term "Lady Bird Deed" of course was much easier to remember than Enhanced Life Estate Deed, so it stuck. Although, Claudia Alta Johnson never did use a "Lady Bird Deed".

This particular deed allows your mother to transfer the ownership of her home, but she retains the right to sell the property, keep the proceeds, and live in the property. Under the law, this is not considered a transfer for Medicaid or Federal Tax purposes.

Additionally, effective as of September 1st, 2015, Texas allows property to be transferred upon one's death through a deed known as the Transfer on Death Deed (TODD). (This law is codified under Chapter 114 of the Texas Estate Code.) The code specifically states that it was not intended to affect other ways of transferring property like the Enhanced Life Estate Deed. The following are relevant provisions of a TODD:

1. It is revocable by the Grantor as long as the Grantor has the mental capacity;
2. It cannot be created through the use of a power of attorney;
3. It must be recorded in the county where the real property is located;
4. It does not require consideration to be effective;
5. A will does not revoke a TODD;
6. A final judgement of a court dissolving the marriage revokes a previously created TODD;
7. It does not affect the ad valorem tax exemptions, including exemptions for residence homestead, persons 65 years of age or older, persons with disabilities, and veterans;
8. It doesn't affect an interest or right of a secured or unsecured creditor of your mother;
9. It doesn't affect your mother's eligibility for any public assistance;
10. It doesn't trigger the "due on sale" or similar clauses in a mortgage;
11. It doesn't invoke a statutory real estate notice or disclosure requirements;
12. It doesn't create a legal or equitable interest in favor of the designated beneficiary; and

13. It doesn't subject your mother's property to claims or creditors of the beneficiaries.

Commonly, I get asked the question: "should I do a TODD or an Enhanced Life Estate Deed?" As you can see above, the TODD has numerous codified benefits. As a general rule, it makes sense to use a TODD unless you're going to have to sign a TODD through a power of attorney, or you anticipate that you may need to revoke the TODD after a grantor has become incapacitated. However, all in all, the numerous codified benefits seem to outweigh the Enhanced Life Estate Deed.

Transfer on Death Car Title (Beneficiary Designation for a Motor Vehicle)

On September 1 2015, The Texas State Legislature passed a law allowing for the transfer on death designation of a motor vehicle; the actual name of the form is VTR-121 Beneficiary Designation for a Motor Vehicle. This document can be found online by going to this link https://www.txdmv.gov/.../8516-vtr-121-beneficiary-designation-for-a-motor-vehicle. As this law was passed at the same time as the Transfer on Death Deed, many individuals tend to search for this document under the name Transfer on Death Title.

There is also another document which can be used to transfer ownership of a vehicle under rights of survivorship laws. This document is Texas Form VTR-122 and you can access the document at this link

http://www.txdmv.gov/publications-tac/doc_download/1994-vtr-122-
rights-of-survivorship-ownership-agreement-for-a-motor-vehicle. If you
have a joint owner on the vehicle, for instance a spouse, you will use this
document to transfer ownership.

This new law is codified under Texas Estate Code chapter 115; below are
some of the details you need to know regarding this particular law:

1. The form is revocable;
2. A trust can be a beneficiary; (Chapter 115 uses Section 311.005 of
   the Government Code);
3. It is a non-testamentary instrument; (should avoid the Medicaid
   Estate Recovery Program);
4. A Last Will and Testament will not revoke this beneficiary
   designation;
5. A beneficiary may disclaim this inheritance under chapter 240 of the
   Texas Property Code;
6. A spouse will have to agree to the transfer of a non-spouse;
7. A beneficiary must survive 120 hours to inherit;
8. Creditor claims still attach to property which has transferred to a
   beneficiary.

These two forms are simple estate planning tools that can help properly
structure an estate plan.

CHAPTER 18: REDUCING RECOVERY THROUGH DOCUMENTATION

Texas Administrative Code § 373.213 allows for the deduction of expenses, home maintenance, and costs of care from Texas MERP. The Code gives the following deductions (AS LONG AS DOCUMENTION IS PROVIDED):

1. Your mother's home expenses and taxes for maintaining the home;

2. Your mother's utility bills, insurance, home repairs, and lawn care;

3. Costs for care (including payments for personal attendant care) provided that those services allow your mother not to be institutionalized;

Keep all of the receipts showing exactly what was spent on your mother given the above guidelines. After she passes away, you need to make this request within 60 days after receiving the Notice of Intent to file a Claim by MERP. All supporting documentation must be attached to the request and sent to MERP, Home Maintenance/Costs of Care Request, P.O. Box 13247, Austin, Texas 78711.

PART FIVE: MEDICARE, VA BENEFITS & MEDICAID APPLICATION PROCESS

CHAPTER 19: MEDICARE NURSING HOME BENEFIT

I f your mother was to go to a skilled nursing home, Medicare Part A includes 100 days if all of the following requirements are met:

1. It must be a "skilled care" facility. There are different types of care such as "custodial" or "intermediary."
2. The Skilled Nursing Facility (SNF) must be preceded by a hospital inpatient stay of at least three consecutive days, not counting the day your mother was discharged;
   a. Example: If your mother came to the emergency room and spent one day there and then two days in the hospital as an inpatient, she would not meet the requirement because her first day in the Emergency Room was not considered inpatient care.
   b. Example: If she came to the same hospital but she was admitted to the hospital for three days and discharged on the fourth, she would then meet the 3-day inpatient requirement.
3. Admission to the SNF must occur within 30 days after discharge from the hospital, unless it would be medically inappropriate.

Medicare does not pay everything for the full 100 days, rather, it will pay the following:

1. Days 1-20: Full cost
2. Days 21-100: Your mother will have to pay the copayment of $167.50 a day. The co-payment usually exceeds the private pay costs in Texas. However, your mother's Medicare Supplement Insurance should cover the copayment. If she is eligible for the QMB, then that will cover the cost.
3. Day 101 and beyond: All costs are on your mother.

Your mother can actually reset the time by remaining out of either hospital care or "skilled" nursing care for 60 continuous days. After this period, the time starts again and she can get the same benefit as long as the above requirements are met.

Medicare Prescription Drug Coverage ("Part D")

If your mother qualifies for Medicaid Long-term care or under a Community Based Alternative program, a benefit which she can receive is payment in full of her prescription medication (s). Your mother may qualify for this benefit even if she is subject to the penalty period for a transfer.

In order for this to happen however, your mother will need to have a Medicare Drug Plan. Please do one of the following:

1. Go to https://www.medicare.gov/find-a-plan/questions/home.aspx.

2. Complete a paper enrollment form at https://www.medicare.gov/sign-up-change-plans/get-drug-coverage/get-drug-coverage.html.
3. Call the plan provider
4. Call Medicare at 1-800-633-4227 (1-800-MEDICARE)

The Medicare Hospice Election

Since 1983, Medicare has covered the cost of hospice. This is one of the most generous benefits provided by Medicare, as with it, your mother may receive full medical support. Whether being cared for in her own home or temporarily at an inpatient facility or hospital, she can choose a hospice election as long as the following conditions are met:

1. She has Medicare Part A hospital insurance;
2. Her primary physician and the hospice physician sign a statement identifying at least one terminal condition (Terminal condition means that she is expected to die within 6 months if it runs its normal course);
3. Your mother or her representative signs a statement waiving the right to treatment of the terminal condition; and
4. Enroll in a hospice program that is approved by Medicare.

Medicare hospice benefits will cover a number of critical resources, including: doctor and nurse care, medical equipment and supplies, medication to control pain, home health aides, dietary counseling, grief and loss counseling for family members. In addition, it will pay for short-term hospital and nursing home care.

CHAPTER 20: QUALIFIED MEDICARE BENEFICIARY PROGRAM

The Qualified Medicare Beneficiary (QMB) Program is designed to assist your mother by paying her:

1. Medicare Part B premium;
   a. Medicare Part B premiums are based upon your mother income reported on her taxes 2 years ago. Most likely she is the lowest amount of $134 a month. However, it can be as high as $428.60 a month.
2. Medicare copayments and deductibles;
   a. Once your mother meets her deductible she will be required to pay the coinsurance of 20% of the Medicare-approved amount charged by providers for her health care services.

In addition to the above assistance, your mother will automatically qualify for Medicare Part D "Extra Help." The Extra Help program is estimated to be worth about $4,900 a year. If your mother does not qualify for QMB, she may want to apply for Extra Help for assistance. The requirements are as follows (in 2018):

1. She must reside in the United States;
2. Her resources must be limited to $14,100 for an individual and $28,150 for a married couple living together. Resources are the same rules as we have discussed throughout this book.

3. Her annual income must be limited to $18,210 for an individual and $24,690 for a married couple living together. If your mother makes more than this, she still might qualify. If you would like to apply your mother for this program, you can do it online at www.socialsecurity.gov/extrahelp or call Social Security at 1-800-772-1213.

The requirements to qualify for QMB are as follows:

1. Your mother's income is limited to $1,025 if she is single and $1,374 if she is married;
2. Her resource limit is $7,390 if single and $11,090 if she is married.

Since the income requirements are so low there is no transfer penalty to become eligible for this program. However, if your mother was to go into a nursing home or a Community Based Alternative program she would be subject to the penalty period. The income requirements are not as strict in that you can receive help from other family members as long as they pay a provider directly.

To apply for this program, you can visit https://www.benefits.gov/benefits/benefit-details/6177. For any more information that you may need please call 1-800-633-4227. It does not hurt to apply if you believe that you qualify.

CHAPTER 21: VA BENEFITS

This book's primary focus is on Medicaid Long-term care Benefits and strategies which can be implemented to protect your mother's estate. The only other program offered through the Federal Government which can assist with long-term care are VA benefits. Here is a brief discussion of each program offered by the VA:

Aid & Attendance (A&A)

Aid & Attendance monthly pension amount may be added to your mother's monthly pension if she meets one of the following conditions:

1. Your mother requires the aid of another person in order to perform the functions of everyday living, such as bathing, feeding, dressing, attending to the wants of nature, adjusting prosthetic devices, or protecting herself from the hazards of her daily environment.

2. Your mother is bedridden, in that her disability requires that she remains in bed.

3. Your mother is living in a nursing facility due to mental or physical incapacity.

4. Your mother's eyesight is limited to a corrected 5/200 visual acuity or less in both eyes; or concentric contraction of the visual field to 5 degrees or less.

Housebound

In addition, an increased monthly pension may be given if your mother is substantially confined to her premises because of a permanent disability. There is another government-based program available through the Veterans Administration. This book really isn't designed to offer an in-depth analysis of this program, but understand that the following eligibility requirements are in place in order to determine if your mother can even seek these benefits:

1. Your mother or her spouse was discharged from service under other than dishonorable conditions, and

2. Your mother or her spouse served 90 days or more of active duty with at least 1 day during a period of wartime (see the definition of wartime below), and

3. If your mother is using her spouse's VA benefit, she did not remarry after the spouse's death, and

4. Your mother's countable income is within the following tables limits:

Veteran Family Status	Basic Pension Income Limit	Housebound Income Limit	Aid & Attendance Income Limit
Veteran with no dependents	$13,166	$16,089	$21,962

Veteran with a non-veteran spouse or child (add $2,250 per child)	$17,241	$20,166	$26,036
Surviving Spouse/Death Pension	$8,830	$10,792	$14,133

5.   For Aid & Attendance: Your mother is disabled and needs to receive that level of income necessary for "assistance on a regular basis to protect [her] from hazards or dangers in [her] daily environment." If your mother is in a nursing facility, the VA presumes she has need for "aid and attendance."

One very important rule is the requirement to serve during wartime. The wartime requirement is determined by Congress; the following are considered periods of war:

1. *World War I.* April 6, 1917, through November 11, 1918, inclusive. If the veteran served with the United States military forces in Russia, the ending date is April 1, 1920. Service after November 11, 1918 and before July 2, 1921 is considered World War I service if the veteran served in the active military, naval, or air service after April 5, 1917 and before November 12, 1918.

2. *World War II.* December 7, 1941, through December 31, 1946, inclusive. If the veteran was in service on December 31, 1946, continuous service before July 26, 1947, is considered World War II service.

3. *Korean conflict.* June 27, 1950, through January 31, 1955, inclusive.

4. *Vietnam era.* The period beginning on February 28, 1961, and ending on May 7, 1975, inclusive, in the case of a veteran who served in the Republic of Vietnam during that period. The period beginning on August 5, 1964, and ending on May 7, 1975, inclusive, in all other cases. 38 U.S.C. 101(29).

5. *Persian Gulf War.* The period beginning on August 2, 1990 and ending on the date thereafter prescribed by Presidential proclamation or by law. 38 U.S.C. 101(33) Note: Different rules apply to this war.

Unfortunately, the VA pension is not a great benefit for your mother if she is on Medicaid and in a nursing home. In that case, her pension is reduced to $90 per month. She may retain the $90 as a personal needs allowance, in addition to the $60 that any Medicaid beneficiary can keep out of his or her own income.

As of September 1st, 2018, VA has no transfer penalty rule, meaning your mother can gift away her property. VA rules on resources are not given; however, generally the calculation is between $30,000 to $80,000. These rules may change in the future, so you should always talk to an attorney.

How to Apply

Your mother can apply for Aid & Attendance or Housebound benefits by writing to the Pension Management Center (PMC) located at the address below for the State of Texas:

St. Paul VA Regional Office

Department of Veterans Affairs
Claims Intake Center
Attention: St. Paul Pension Center
PO BOX 5365
Janesville, WI 53547-5365
Fax: 1-844-655-1604

In addition, you can get even more localized help by going to https://www.benefits.va.gov/waco/. This office services most of Texas. There is another office in Houston; you can go to their webpage at https://www.benefits.va.gov/houston/.

Always remember that government employees want to help your mother, but they need documentation. Please gather all doctor reports validating the need for A&A or Housebound care. In addition, they will need to see all financial documentation. DO NOT LIE TO THE GOVERNMENT.

CHAPTER 22: MEDICAID APPLICATION PROCESS

As of 2018, because of the complexity and some of the confusion when it comes to applying for Medicaid Long Term Care, a large number of applications tend to get wrongfully denied. Attempts have been made to correct this problem like the implementation of "Business Process Redesign" (BPR), but there are still many things that need to be fixed. What you most definitely want to do is to make sure that everything is organized and easy to navigate for the HHSC staff.

HHSC accepts applications for Medicaid Long-term care in three ways:

1. Online filing: YourTexasBenefits.com;
2. By Fax: 1-877-447-2839
3. Filing a hard copy: mail to HHSC P.O. Box 149024, Austin, Texas 78714-9024

If you feel overwhelmed with the process, then hire an attorney to assist you. An attorney will have access to special help without having to go through an appeal process.

The following is a checklist of items you'll need to apply for Medicaid Long-term care for your mother:

CHECKLIST OF ITEMS NEEDED

- ☐ Copy of Power of Attorney documents
- ☐ Copy of your mother's photo ID
- ☐ Your mother's Medicare card
- ☐ Supplemental health insurance cards
- ☐ Social Security Card
- ☐ Birth Certificate
- ☐ Marriage License
- ☐ Verification of health insurance premiums
- ☐ All Life Insurance Policies
- ☐ All prepaid funeral contracts and burial policies (make sure they are irrevocable)
- ☐ Verification of All Income: Social Security stubs, pension/retirement checks, civil service, VA benefits, annuities, etc.
- ☐ Last 3 months of all checking and saving accounts
- ☐ Current CD statement
- ☐ Current IRA statement
- ☐ Current 401k statement
- ☐ Current brokerage account statement
- ☐ All stock certificates or account statements
- ☐ All mutual funds
- ☐ Most recent Tax assessment for all real property
- ☐ All deeds to real estate owned

Lastly, a very important piece of information you must provide to Medicaid Long-term care is documentation showing all of the transfers your mother has made in the past five years. I understand this might be difficult, but you are required by law to provide this when applying for Medicaid.

PART SIX: PREPARE FOR YOUR FUTURE.

CHAPTER 23: THE LONG-TERM CARE CONDUNRUM

By: Jeffery Reddick, CFP

As you can see using government benefits is incredibly complicated and it will only become more and more complicated in the future. Many of the loopholes which are available today, will not be there in the future. In fact, if we don't find new solutions quick, we might not even have a Medicaid program of the future. Proper Estate Planning is critical in the protection and preservation of wealth as they relate to a long-term care event. If not done correctly, bankruptcy in your retirement years, can progressively become a financial burden on your children and grandchildren. No one wishes for a significant accident or illness to befall them, but it is essential to plan for these contingencies nonetheless.

All people face three primary financial risks as it relates to the financial health of their family:

1. Failure to preserve enough resources for a long life;
2. Dying before you had the ability to create enough resources for your family; and
3. Unforeseen disability which exhausts resources faster than you anticipated.

On the face of it, risks 2 and 3 are obvious, but number 1 doesn't seem so intuitive. How do you live too long? Well, from a financial perspective if you outlive the resources you have for retirement, this is the financial industries definition of "living too long".

Failure to preserve enough resources for a long life:

An individual addresses this risk of living too long by saving and investing properly. The government goes to great length to offer incentives to those who will save for the future. The reason is because it is so unnatural. Homo Sapiens are the only species who preserve resources for more than a year; and within our own species, almost 80% fail to save enough resources for their later years.

This book will not go in-depth into the hundreds of strategies available to save for retirement. For example, a simple strategy to avoid outliving your assets is setting up a private pension, commonly known as an annuity. Annuities over the years has received a bad reputation from media outlets and fee only financial advisor; but an annuity like any other product can be bad, okay, good or great. It just requires a little research and education to understand what you are purchasing.

Dying before you had the ability to create enough resources for your family.

If you were to pass too soon, you haven't had enough time to accumulate assets so that your family can replace the income you earn. This doesn't mean that you pass at a young age. Like it was explained at the beginning of this book, resources are not distributed equally across society. Therefore, some people can work a lifetime and never create enough resources for their family. This is the primary risk that traditional life insurance was designed to solve.

Unforeseen disability which exhausts resources faster than you anticipated:

Becoming disabled may be a more detrimental financial situation than even a death. So, a disability brings with it all the financial impact as if a person had died, plus the additional cost of care, therapy, rehabilitation and basic living expenses of the disabled person. This is what disability insurance is designed to help with. However, disability insurance just replaces a portion of the income the person was earning, it doesn't pay for any actual cost of care issues.

Effectively, long-term care insurance was intended to be the other half of the equation when someone becomes disabled. The disability insurances would pay the income benefit out, usually sixty to eighty percent of the persons income after a waiting period (qualification period) and, generally, the disability income benefit would continue until the resolution of the disability or retirement age, whichever comes first.

Long-term care insurance would kick in simultaneously, if the individual had it, either as a group benefit or as an individually owned policy. So, to protect you and your family from these three primary risks one saves and invests properly, and then buys life insurance, disability insurance, and long-term care insurance to cover their risk. Simple right? Not so fast, the devil is in the details.

The first generation of long-term care policies that came about in the 1980's were very limited in scope and were in effect nursing home policies. These where primarily bought by the generation of the great depression/greatest generation and were not well received by the public, particularly when it came time for claims. Receiving your benefit was often a prolonged, arduous task as the benefits of the policy were so stringent that many people had legitimate long-term care situations that their policies simply didn't cover. This was an inherent, but poorly understood by the consumer, flaw in these "nursing home only" policies. As a matter of fact, it is a common misconception to think that one would only need the benefits of a long-term care policy if they were in a nursing home.

Two disturbing facts will quickly disabuse anyone of this notion:

1. Forty percent of all long-term care is provided to people under the age of 65.
2. Eight percent of all long-term care is provided for outside of nursing homes. Primarily in-home care or at assisted living facilities.

As you can see, you can spend a lot of money on care and never even enter a nursing home and as it has been demonstrated throughout this book Medicaid Long-Term Care is designed for nursing home care not for assisted living facilities and personal home care.

The next generation of long-term care insurance was meant to address these issues and woo the baby boomer generation. These second-generation policies were much broader in scope and offered much richer benefits. In the late 1990s to early 2000s, a healthy, non-smoking married couple in their late fifties or early sixties could get a policy that would pay out $4,000 to $5,000 a month, per person, for life (plus inflation) for an annual cost of $3,000 to $5,000 a year. Not inexpensive to be sure, but less than the cost of one month of care in an average assisted living facility.

The benefits would be triggered if the insured suffered from the loss of function of two of the six ADLs (Activities of Daily Living: dressing, bathing, transferring, toileting, continence, and eating); or, suffered from a mental impairment: Alzheimer's, dementia, and Parkinson's disease to name a few. A massive wave of soon to be retirees, flush with cash from the 1980s and 1990s bull market were ripe for the picking. Virtually every major insurance company in the US rolled out a long-term care policy in the 1990's. This was to be the insurance market of the 21st century. Barely twenty-years later and ninety-five percent of these companies don't even offer these kinds of policies anymore. Why is that? What happened? Didn't these companies want to sell these policies? The answer is they did, until they didn't.

Insurance companies found out that while this is a huge market, making money in that market is much more difficult. Two primary factors from the end of the 1990's until today turned the long-term care market from one of great potential to one that virtually no insurance company wanted a part of, at least not in the form of these second-generation policies.

Factor one: Cost of care went through, and continues to go through, double digit inflation. This will have an endpoint as eventually the cost of care will be so exorbitant as no one can afford it. Still, the insurance companies never imagined that care would get so expensive so quickly. This meant that for the average client to cover their risk, they would have to buy higher and higher coverage policies. Many people, if they can't afford to cover their risk fully, would just choose not to buy. A married couple who might be able to get coverage for $4,000 a year ten years ago, might now have to spend $4,000 to $5,000 per person, or more (presuming they bought at the same age) to have a similar benefit and even then, the benefits were likely to not be as robust. Hence, because the care industry got more expensive, so did the policies, leaving many potential customers behind.

Factor two: Lapse ratios collapsed. That's insurance speak for virtually every policy sold stayed on the books (especially in the early years when insurance companies weren't charging enough to cover the costs of the benefits that would be paid out in the long run just to gain market share). This is a problem for insurance companies. For insurance to work many people need to buy it, but only some people need to use it. The baby boomer generation, having seen their parents struggle with cost of care, held on to these policies with an iron grip. For example: Let's assume an insurance company sold 100 long-term care policies to a group of 60-year-old clients and lets further assume that they knew that no one would use the policy until age seventy and at age seventy, only fifty of the hundred policies sold would still be in-force. Furthermore, of those fifty policies only ten would be paying claims. The rest had been cancelled, or lapsed; because of death, or divorce, or the client went to another company, or perhaps they just didn't want or could no longer afford the coverage. It doesn't matter, there are a myriad of reasons why this might occurred. It happens in every industry companies experience attrition in their customer base. As time passes some of the insurance companies' customers/clients from any given year just go away. In the insurance world this is called the lapse ratio. This is a very important number to get right because it directly effects how the insurance industry price the policy and how much coverage the company is on the hook for. If the lapse ratio is too high, insurance companies don't have enough revenue to operate the business. If the lapse ratio is too low, insurance companies have too many future claims.

Many of the biggest and best life insurance companies, which also were the primary issuers of long-term care insurance, have well over 100 years' experience in, pricing, issuing and maintaining life insurance policies. They have the lapse ratios down to a science. And since this was a new niche in the insurance industry, they looked to their deep life insurance experience to figure out how to underwrite and price long-term care policies. This turned out, in hindsight, to be a huge mistake.

So, let's go back to the example: If only fifty policies of the hundred initially sold 10 years ago are still in force, that represents a lapse ratio of 5%. And, according to our example only 20% of the remaining policies, or

10 actual policies, are paying claims. For the insurance company to make money and be competitive in the market place they have to price and underwrite their policies just right so that they make enough money to be able to show a profit after paying for 10 "still on the books" policies that file a claim.

Looking back, insurance companies made two miscalculations:

1. They underestimated what percent of polices would go on claim. For argument sake, in our example, instead of twenty percent of the policies on the books at age seventy filing a claim let's say its forty. That would mean twenty policies out of fifty were on claim, not ten. So, if we assume everything else was done correctly by the insurance company except for this assumption, the insurance company likely charged half as much as they should have to be able to profitably pay these claims.

2. The second, and even greater miscalculation, was once the baby boomers saw the toll and expense of care on their parents they didn't lapse their policies. Instead of experiencing a lapse ratio of our hypothetical 5% annually. The long-term care insurance industry experience lapse ratios closer to 1% annually. Meaning that after ten years, they didn't have fifty policies on the books. They had ninety! And if 40% of ninety file claims were made, now the insurance company is on the hook for literally hundreds of millions of dollars in claims that they never planned.

The result is over the last 10 years almost every major insurance company has gotten out of this market. The ones that are left have made the policies they have so expensive and the benefits so limited, that it has become a joke in the industry that if you can afford a policy you can afford not to have a policy. Unfortunately, the side effect of significantly underestimating cost of care, number of claims, and the lapse ratio, translates to insurance companies being forced to raise rates on the consumers who had purchased these policies. These rate increase have been as much as 80%. In one year! Note, this isn't the insurance companies being greedy. To raise rates on a entire group of policies you have to prove to the insurance regulators that rate increase is absolutely necessary to maintain the financial solvency of the book of business. This was a last resort move to try and staunch the bleeding for the sky-high claims they are experiencing for policies sold in the 1990s and early to mid-2000s. Few, if any, major insurance companies have escaped this fate. As a result, most insurance companies no longer offer long-term care policies of this type. They just can't profitably solve the equation of how to price these policies.

Which brings us to today. Most people cannot afford to handle the potential financial risk of a long-term care event in their family without it wreaking havoc on their retirement funds, if not wiping them out entirely. A lengthy long-term care scenario is the single biggest risk the average retiree faces. But as we have just demonstrated the obvious solution, traditional long-term care insurance, doesn't seem to solve the problem anymore. The policies that are still available are so expensive as to be prohibitive and even if you can afford them there is no guarantee that after you have paid in years of premium they won't raise the rates beyond what you can afford (or want to pay) sometime in the future. So, what is a prudent, planning person to do?

CHAPTER 24: LONG-TERM CARE SOLUTIONS

P rudent long-term care planning is the available legal asset protection and strategies available so an individual can minimize the amount of assets exposed to loss in the case of an adverse long-term care event.

There are three options available to protect your estate from a long-term care event:

1. **Self-Fund**: Most nursing home facilities provide their monthly costs online. Projecting a 7% increase in medical cost per year, a person can determine if they have enough assets to provide for their own care. This is a most used option but not realistic for many.

2. **Government Based Long-Term Care**: You just read a whole book about this. Hopefully, you are familiar with the concept by now.

3. **A Hybrid Long-Term Care Solution**: A hybrid solution is the current generation of long-term care insurance as offered by the insurance industry which allows life insurance to be paid early for a long-term care event.

In practical terms, most hybrid long-term care policies are a form of permanent life insurance (whole, universal, index, or variable) that will advance a percentage of the death benefit to the insured, tax free, if they

141

meet the qualifications of the long-term care event. What this simply means is that the insured has access to the vast majority of their death benefit while they are alive. This is an improvement on the long-term care policies of old which provided daily or monthly benefits for a period of years or even for life. The benefit to the insured is access to a significant asset when and if they need it. However, if they have a healthy and long retirement without significant medical complications and don't need long-term care, they can pass on the death benefit to their loved ones and they do not have to keep a large sum reserved for the future "what if "scenario.

The primary challenge of self-funding long-term care is resource availability. Many Americans hold hundreds of thousands of dollars in IRAs and investment accounts and live in utter poverty because they don't know if they will need the resources in the future. If they would give up the idea that they need to self-fund their long-term care and use a hybrid policy, the insured can put a policy enforce for pennies on the dollar of the eventual benefits used. If they never have a long-term care situation, their loved ones, or a charitable concern, can benefit from the value of the policy upon death. Also, if the policy has a cash value, and they get to a point, for whatever reason, that they aren't concerned about funding a long-term care event, they could always cash out the policy and enjoy those proceeds in their retirement. Of course, last but not least, if they have a long-term care event, they simply put a claim in against the policy and receive the benefit they are entitled to.

Many hybrid policies will allow for up to 90% of the death benefit to be forwarded to the insured if they qualify for two of the six activities of daily living or have a mental impairment. Often these benefits are paid out annually, as a lump sum, to the insured to be used however they wish.

So, a seventy-year old man who is diagnosed with Alzheimer's who has a one-million-dollar lift/long-term care hybrid policy could receive, tax free, 20% of the policy face amount ($200,000 per year up to a total of $900,000 over 4 years). Whatever amount of the policy death benefit is not used while the man is alive would pass to heirs, also tax free.

You can see how this is a more attractive solution for most people as they are guaranteed one of the following:
1. they can cash out their policy and keep the value of the policy;
2. they could use the death benefit for long-term care event; ot
3. they can have the death benefit pay out to their loved ones or a charity.

In each situation the insured gets value for the premiums they've paid.

A life insurance company is required by law to pay out more than they receive if a insured pays all their premium payments. Why would the insurance company offer a product like this? Quite simply, this generation of long-term care policies puts the insurance companies back in control in two ways:

1. They get back to a pricing model they understand…life insurance. History shows they are much better at the proper pricing life insurance policies versus traditional long-term care policies.

2. They limit their risk exposure to a pre-determined maximum payout. They know, at issue of the policy, what their max loss can be…the death benefit. Many early long-term care policies had unlimited years of benefits on the policy along with inflation riders of five percent or more. By making the long-term care benefit and the death benefit one and the same, the insurance industry took much of the "guess work" out of how to price a long-term care insurance.

There are many strategies that an estate planning attorney, often working in concert with a skilled financial planner, can put in place to help ensure that wealth is preserved and aren't exposed to financial hurricanes that a significant long-term care even can create. Even for those who have the resources to absorb any potential future costs, the concept of good stewardship would suggest that these planning strategies still have value.

For my clients, who upon first reflection, suggest they will just "write a check" if need be, I ask them a simple question: Do you carry full coverage car insurance? The answer is always, without fail, of course. Why? Some of course respond because I have to because the law requires but most understand that they can just write a check. If they happened to be in a car accident they want someone else to handle the situation…the insurance company.

A common strategy for people who have assets outside of an IRA, is to create an irrevocable trust that owns hybrid long-term care policies. A gift can be made into the trust purchasing an annuity that then funds the life/long-term care policy in perpetuity. If there is need for the long-term care portion of the coverage, the benefit can be paid out to the insured. If the insured does not need to use the long-term care portion, the death benefit of the policy will pass onto the beneficiaries.

Unfortunately, in the financial planning industry, there are many concerns about purchasing a life insurance policy. The three biggest concerns are: (1) the cost of the insurance, (2) ability the client has to keep paying the premium, and (3) the policy covers an insured long-term care event.

The Cost of Insurance

Insurance agents are paid a commission to sale insurance products. While this is not wrong per se, the way the insurance agent is paid does create a conflict of interest. An insurance agent is paid a commission based upon the cost of insurance not upon the performance of the policy. The more the client pays, the more the insurance agent get paid. To alleviate this issue, many financial planner firms have switched to a fee-only financial planning practice. This means the advisor only gets paid a percentage of assets under management. While this appears to be a good idea, an adverse effect has taken place. Many advisors underinsure their clients because they do not want to take away from assets which could be under management. In all honesty, the only way to resolve this issue is to take the time to understand that your cost of insurance is based upon three things: (1) your expected life span, (2) the amount of insurance, and (3) the benefits that you receive. The longer your life the less the cost of insurance. The more the death benefit, the greater the cost. If you're a smoker, then you are going to pay more. Taking the time to really understand the cost will help you greatly determine if the product is for you.

Ability the Client Has to Keep Paying the Premium

I will have many clients who have paid years on a policy to only get to retirement unable to pay the premium. This is really unfortunate planning. Usually in my planning sessions, the goal is to have the policy fully funded within seven years, so my clients do not need to make any payments later in life. This is not always possible but when it is, it is the best course of action.

The Policy Covers an Insured Long-Term Care Event

The most frustrating thing for any insurance product is to find out when you go to use it that you are not insured for that event. For example, a common situation people face is that an individual purchases car insurance and finds out that they did not get underinsured coverage, or they did not get enough insurance. With a hybrid policy it is understanding what you are really covered for in a long-term care event. Taking time to talk to your insurance agent about what you are really covered for and making sure that it is written in the policy is extremely important.

Hopefully, as you have read this book and experienced your mother's long-term care needs, you take the time to prepare for your future. It takes time and money but purchasing good insurance can drastically affect where you will live and what type of care you will receive.

54130095R00083

Made in the USA
Columbia, SC
26 March 2019